VINEYARD
SEASONS

No matter what
the seasons be
My books bring
sunshine home to me.

"THEREFORE ALL SEASONS SHALL BE SWEET TO THEE..."

♥ Samuel Taylor Coleridge

"One morning we ran into a
neighbor at the store and she
asked brightly,
    'What was it at your house?'
'Fourteen below,' we replied.
Her face fell. 'We had minus
twelve,' she said, and you
could see that her day was ruined."

♥ Richard Ketchum

A TIME TO EVERY PURPOSE UNDER HEAVEN

VINEYARD SEASONS

MORE FROM THE
HEART
OF THE
HOME

BY
SUSAN
BRANCH

LITTLE, BROWN AND COMPANY

BOSTON   TORONTO

FIRST EDITION

Library of Congress Cataloging-in-Publication Data
Branch, Susan.
   Vineyard seasons.

   Includes index.
   1. Cookery.   2. Entertaining.   I. Title.
   TX715.B8176   1988   641.5   88~9984
   ISBN 0~316~10632~1

♡ Excerpt from "Symptom Recital" in The Portable Dorothy Parker. Copyright 1926, renewed © 1954 by Dorothy Parker. Reprinted by permission of Viking Penguin, Inc.
♥ Excerpt from Grapefruit by Yoko Ono. Copyright ©1964, 1970 by Yoko Ono. Reprinted by permission of Simon and Schuster, Inc.
♡ Excerpt from "The Look" in Collected Poems by Sara Teasdale. Copyright 1915 by Macmillan Publishing Company, renewed 1943 by Mamie T. Wheless. Reprinted by permission of Macmillan Publishing Company.

HC: 10 9 8 7 6 5 4 3 2 1

Published simultaneously in Canada (♥) by Little, Brown and Company (Canada) Limited

PRINTED IN THE UNITED STATES OF AMERICA

Sue

Jim

Steve

FOR MOM

This is a surprise for my mother:
these little pictures of her
fabulous children & this dedication.
    Because of my creative mother I became
proficient at many wonderful things: I can twirl the baton &
I'm a wicked jacks player (tho' never as wicked as she!). I know the
very best lagger for hopscotch & all the best hide-
& go-seek places on Claire Avenue. I speak
"Arf & Arfy" fluently, know games to play
on babies' faces & can sing the words to
wonderful songs that no one else ever
heard of. She ordered "Rock Around
the Clock" from American Bandstand
& taught us how to dance, tightened my roller skates with a key
before I went out & helped us put on a circus complete with
"Man   Eating Tigers" (one of my brothers sitting behind a
curtain eating animal crackers).
    Her patience was never-ending,
her heart is gold & I love
her, my mom, Patricia
Louise Stewart. ♥

Chuck

Brad

Paula

Mary

Shelly

P.S. I want no flak from you kids
about these pictures... I did my
best! ♥

CONTENTS

"A little house — a house of my own —
Out of the wind's and the rain's way."
♥ Padraic Colum

APPETIZERS

"It is extraordinary how music sends one
back into memories of the past — and it
is the same with smells."

George Sand ♥

STEAK TARTARE
Makes 2 cups

The beef should be partially frozen when ground, so it will be icy cold when served. It's good to set the serving dish in a bowl of ice. ♥

1 lb. beef tenderloin, partially frozen
3 Tbsp. minced onion
2 Tbsp. minced parsley
6 shakes Tabasco sauce
1½ tsp. Worcestershire sauce
4 tsp. capers
freshly ground black pepper, to taste
½ tsp. ruby port
pumpernickel cocktail bread
sweet butter

Cut beef into 1" cubes ~ grind in food processor 6~8 seconds. Combine onion, parsley, Tabasco, Worcestershire, capers, pepper & port; then stir in beef. Spread pumpernickel slices with sweet butter and serve alongside the steak tartare. ♥

"He that is of a merry heart hath
a continual feast."
♥ Proverbs 15:15

SALMON-STUFFED PUMPERNICKEL

Great for a buffet. ♥

½ lb. smoked salmon
1 8-oz. pkg cream cheese
3 green onions
2 tsp. Worcestershire
2 tbsp. fresh lemon juice
½ c. milk

½ tsp. Tabasco
¼ c. capers, drained
1 whole, round loaf
    pumpernickel
1 pkg. pumpernickel
    cocktail bread

Put first 7 ingredients into food processor & blend till smooth. Stir in capers. Cover & refrigerate until ready to serve. Cut the top off the round loaf of pumpernickel bread & hollow it out. Fill with salmon mixture & serve with cocktail bread. ♥

" . . . our life is what our
thoughts make it."
    ♥ Marcus Aurelius

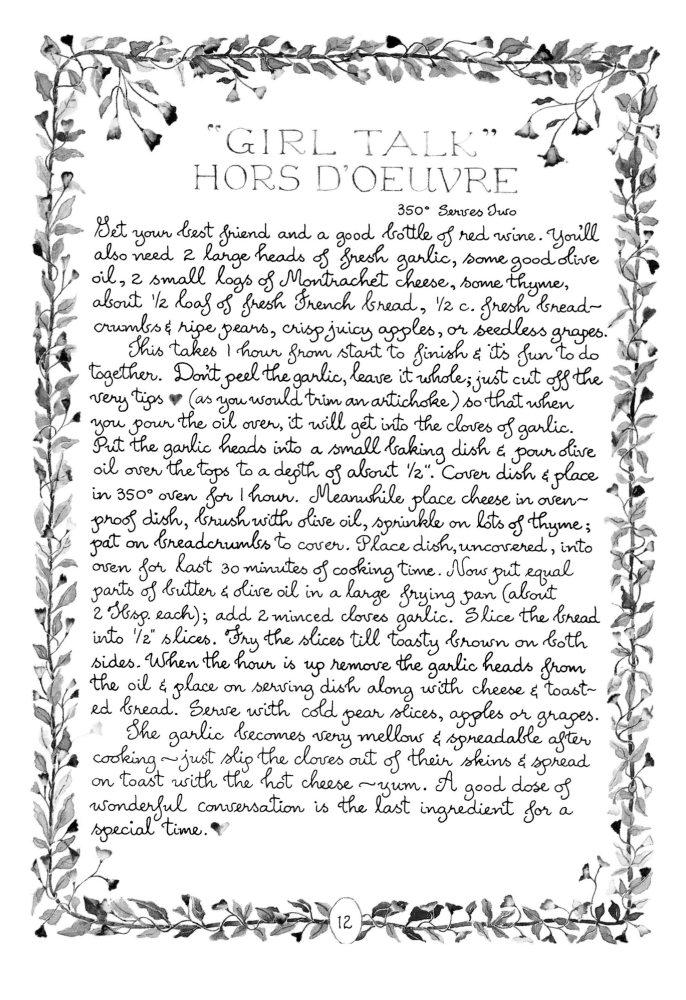

"GIRL TALK" HORS D'OEUVRE

350° Serves Two

Get your best friend and a good bottle of red wine. You'll also need 2 large heads of fresh garlic, some good olive oil, 2 small logs of Montrachet cheese, some thyme, about ½ loaf of fresh French bread, ½ c. fresh bread-crumbs & ripe pears, crisp juicy apples, or seedless grapes.

This takes 1 hour from start to finish & it's fun to do together. Don't peel the garlic, leave it whole; just cut off the very tips ♥ (as you would trim an artichoke) so that when you pour the oil over, it will get into the cloves of garlic. Put the garlic heads into a small baking dish & pour olive oil over the tops to a depth of about ½". Cover dish & place in 350° oven for 1 hour. Meanwhile place cheese in oven~proof dish, brush with olive oil, sprinkle on lots of thyme; pat on breadcrumbs to cover. Place dish, uncovered, into oven for last 30 minutes of cooking time. Now put equal parts of butter & olive oil in a large frying pan (about 2 Tbsp. each); add 2 minced cloves garlic. Slice the bread into ½" slices. Fry the slices till toasty brown on both sides. When the hour is up remove the garlic heads from the oil & place on serving dish along with cheese & toast-ed bread. Serve with cold pear slices, apples or grapes.

The garlic becomes very mellow & spreadable after cooking ~ just slip the cloves out of their skins & spread on toast with the hot cheese ~ yum. A good dose of wonderful conversation is the last ingredient for a special time. ♥

FONDUE

A fondue is best served as an hors d'oeuvre at a party rather than as a main dish or dessert. It must be kept warm in a chafing dish & I think it adds nice "texture" to the table. ♥

Chocolate   2 cups

I always serve something sweet for balance. ♥

12 oz. semi-sweet chocolate
2/3 c. heavy cream
2 Tbsp. Triple Sec
fruit & cake

Heat the chocolate & cream, stirring over low heat till chocolate melts. Stir in Triple Sec. Keep warm over _very_ low flame; stir occasionally & serve with dipping pieces of bananas, pears, angel food cake, strawberries, pineapple, cherries & apples. ♥

Cheese   2 cups

This is sort of the traditional cheese fondue ~ I sometimes use the cheese sauce in Welsh Rabbit (p. 116) for a change. ♥

1 clove garlic
1 c. dry white wine
8-oz. Gruyère, grated
8-oz. Jarlsberg, grated

2 tsp. cornstarch
3 Tbsp. kirsch
salt, fresh pepper
sprinkle of nutmeg
French bread pieces

Rub a heavy pot with garlic, leaving shreds in pot. Add wine, bring to boil. Add cheeses, lower heat & stir till melted. Dissolve cornstarch in kirsch, add to cheese. Salt & pepper to taste; sprinkle over nutmeg. Keep over _very low_ flame. Serve with bread chunks for dipping, or vegetable pieces. Thin with hot wine if necessary. ♥

YAM CHIPS

Slightly sweet & a nice change. ♥
  3 large yams
  oil for frying
  salt

Peel yams & slice crosswise as thinly as possible. Soak the slices in a big bowl filled with ice & water ½ hr. Drain & thoroughly dry with paper towels. Heat ½" oil in skillet till almost smoking. Fry chips several at a time (don't crowd them) till golden, turning once. Drain on paper towels, blotting to remove excess oil. Salt to taste & serve. ♥

ROASTED FRENCH FRIES

Broiled with a delicious crunch of Parmesan cheese. ♥
  3 large baking potatoes
  ¼ c. melted butter
  Parmesan cheese (grated)
  salt

Don't peel, but cut potatoes into long thin strips. Soak in ice water 1 hour; drain & plunge into boiling water. Cook 5 min. till almost tender. Drain, rinse in cold water, thoroughly pat dry. Preheat broiler. Arrange potatoes on cookie sheet. Brush with melted butter, sprinkle with cheese & salt. Broil about 10 min. till brown & crunchy. Serve. ♥

14

STUFFED GRAPE LEAVES
Makes about 30

This island wasn't named Martha's Vineyard for no reason — wild grapevines are abundant ♥. In the winter we gather the vines to twist & weave into wreaths & in the summer we choose the tenderest leaves to stuff & eat — delicious! (The beautiful green leaves also look wonderful as liners for summer hors d'oeuvre platters, or underneath butter pats on bread plates.) ♥

To gather fresh leaves: of course they must be unsprayed; wild or domestic; clean, whole, flexible & of med. size. Gather & stack them & then, using tongs, dip the stacks in 2 qts. boiling water mixed with 4 tsp. pickling salt for 30 seconds. Drain; gently press out excess moisture. Wrap & freeze or go right on with the recipe. ♥

40 grape leaves, fresh or preserved	1 tsp. cinnamon
1 sm. onion, minced	6 lg. dried prunes, minced
⅓ c. pecans, finely chopped	¼ c. parsley, minced
3 Tbsp. olive oil	2 Tbsp. fresh lemon juice
1½ c. cooked brown rice	Freshly ground pepper

If using preserved leaves, thoroughly rinse in cold water; remove any woody stems. Sauté onion & pecans in oil till onion is tender. Add rice, cinnamon, prunes, parsley, lemon juice, & pepper to taste. Line a heavy pot with grape leaves. On the rest of the leaves put 1 tsp. mixture in the center of each, vein side up. Turn in top of leaf, then sides; roll up. Place in pot, add 1½ c. water. Put a plate on top of them so they stay submerged. Cover the pot & simmer 30 min. Serve cool but not cold. ♥

15

I LOVE NEW YORK

The love of my life has an Aunt Peggy, the youngest 82-year-old I've ever met, who lives in a wonderful old building in New York. We walked over for cocktails on a chilly night in late winter — it was the beginning of a memorable evening that included wonderful stories of sailing on the Queen Elizabeth, of Fred Astaire on stage in 1932, of music by Bobby Short & of watching a beautiful face remember things that could only live in my imagination. It was a step back in time & it began with this little hors d'oeuvre that Peggy had whipped up before our arrival. It just seemed so old-fashioned & New Yorkish to me. It is very simple to prepare & the ingredients can always be kept on hand. You'll need: hard-boiled egg yolks, mayonnaise, capers, minced anchovies, freshly ground pepper & bite-sized toast. Mash the yolks & mix with mayonnaise to make a light paste; add the rest of ingredients to taste & pile on toast. ♥ Pull the curtains, put on some old music, serve your favorite cocktails & dream about what it must have been like to sail to Europe a long time ago. ♥

MONTRACHET WON TONS

Makes 36

Hot, melted Montrachet inside crisp fried wonton skins, & the best thing is they can be cooked & frozen so at "the party" all you have to do is reheat them. ♥

6 oz. cream cheese, softened

2 egg yolks

2 Tbsp. sour cream

2/3 c. Montrachet

2 tsp. thyme

6 Tbsp. shredded Parmesan

2 green onions, minced

salt & pepper

36 wonton wrappers

cornstarch & water to seal

oil for frying

Blend cream cheese, yolks, sour cream, Montrachet, thyme & Parmesan. Stir in onions & salt & pepper to taste. Mix together 1 Tbsp. cornstarch with 1 c. hot water. Wonton wrappers dry out quickly so keep them (finished & unfinished) under a damp cloth. Lay out wonton, dip finger in cornstarch water & brush 4 edges of wonton. Put 1 tsp. filling in center & fold to make a triangle, pressing edges to seal. Bring corners up together, overlap slightly, moisten & pinch together. Fry in 1/4 in. hot oil till browned on all sides. Serve, or cool & freeze. To reheat: do not thaw. Place on cookie sheet & bake in 350° oven for 15 minutes. ♥

Sun-Dried Tomato Bites

425°   Makes 24

Watch out for these; they go fast because they are totally irresistible. ♥

¼ c. olive oil
2 cloves garlic, mashed
1 French-bread baguette
12 oz. Montrachet cheese
¼ c. sour cream
½ tsp. each thyme & rosemary
9 sun-dried tomatoes, coarsely chopped
freshly ground black pepper

Preheat oven to 425°. Crush garlic into olive oil. Thinly slice baguette. Mash Montrachet with enough sour cream to make it spreadable. Add the thyme & rosemary. Chop the tomatoes. Lay the sliced bread on a cookie sheet & brush with garlic oil (one side only). Bake till lightly toasted. Remove from oven & turn them all over. Put a thick layer of the cheese mixture on each, sprinkle on sun-dried tomatoes, grind pepper over all, and bake 3 min., till cheese is melted.   Serve. ♥ Sometimes I serve these with the salad for the first course at dinner. ♥

"Basically my wife was immature. I'd be at home in the bath and she'd come in and sink my boats." ♥ Woody Allen

HOW TO
SUN-DRY TOMATOES

This is a summer occupation, to do when the sun is hot, and the tomatoes ripe and flavorful. There is really nothing to it, yet I have paid as much as $6 for a tiny little jar of them. And they're sooo good! On page 106 you'll find a wonderful recipe for a Sun-Dried Tomato Pesto; I've used them in the delicious Pizza on page 115, & in the appetizer on page 18. They keep indefinitely, which makes them a perfect Christmas gift or a way to bring sunshine to a wintery day.

Use the extra-flavorful Italian tomatoes, plum or Roma. Cover an oven rack with cheesecloth. Cut the tomatoes in half lengthwise & lay them, cut side up, on the cheesecloth. Cover with another piece of cheesecloth. Take them outside & keep them in full sun for 2-3 days, bringing them in at night. They're perfect when dry & shriveled but flexible, not brittle. Pack them sort of loosely in jars & pour over good virgin olive oil to cover. You can add fresh basil leaves or sprigs of rosemary if you like. Cover tightly & keep at room temperature. As I said, they'll keep forever; as long as the oil tastes good & fresh, they're fine ♥.

"Ten measures of speech descended on the world; women took nine and men one." ♥ Babylonian Talmud

SPINACH BALLS ♥

300° Makes 50

Wonderful because they can be made ahead & frozen — just bake as many as you need at a time. You can double & triple this recipe ♥.

2 pkg. frozen chopped spinach   1 chopped onion
4 beaten eggs   1½ tsp. thyme
2 c. herb stuffing (packaged)   3/4 c. butter,
½ c. Parmesan cheese   melted
1 garlic clove, minced   salt & pepper

Cook spinach (according to pkg.); drain & squeeze dry. Mix together all ingredients. Chill for 2 hours. Roll into 1" balls. Freeze on cookie sheet. When frozen, store in plastic bags till needed. Thaw before baking. Bake at 300° for 30 minutes. ♥

20

PESTO "RAVIOLI" WITH WINE SAUCE

Makes 24

This makes an elegant beginning to an Italian dinner. ♥

½ c. ricotta
2 Tbsp. basil pesto ★
24 won ton wrappers
2 Tbsp. butter
2 Tbsp. olive oil
2 cloves garlic, minced

⅓ c. white wine
2 Tbsp. parsley, minced
1 tsp. lemon juice
freshly ground pepper
Parmesan cheese
¼ c. pine nuts, toasted

Mix together ricotta & pesto (there's a recipe for pesto on p. 79 of Heart of the Home). One at a time, put a rounded tsp. of pesto mixture in the center of won ton wrapper. Dip your finger in a glass of water & moisten edges. Fold diagonally; press edges together. Keep finished ones under damp cloth. When all are done, place as many as can fit, without touching, into an oiled steamer basket. Steam over boiling water, covered, 8 min. Remove ravioli with a spatula, one at a time — they will try to stick together. Make the sauce: melt butter in oil. Sauté garlic briefly. Add wine, boil gently 2-3 min. Remove from heat. Stir in parsley & lemon juice. Pour over ravioli. Top with black pepper & toasted pine nuts. ♥

"Manners must adorn knowledge, and smooth its way through the world."
♥ Philip Dormer Stanhope, Earl of Chesterfield

SPINACH DIP

Makes 2+ cups

I have stuffed this mixture into hollowed-out cherry tomatoes & into sugar snap peas. It's perfect as a dip for cut-up fresh vegetables & with all kinds of crackers. ♥

1 10 oz. pkg. chopped spinach,
    thawed & drained
1½ c. sour cream
½ c. mayonnaise
½ c. minced red onion
2 cloves minced garlic
1 Tbsp. fresh lemon juice
½ tsp. hot pepper sauce
¼ tsp. nutmeg

Combine all ingredients; mix well. Cover & chill. ♥

"There is nothing wrong with
the world that a sensible woman
could not settle in an afternoon."
♥ Jean Giraudoux

FORTUNE COOKIES

350° Makes 24

Easy to make and taste better than store-bought (which STILL ain't _that_ great), but the best part is that YOU get to do the fortunes. They can be serious or funny (we have laughed to tears); quote books are a great source for ideas. ♥

3 egg whites   ½ c. cake flour
½ c. white sugar   ½ tsp. vanilla
¼ c. brown sugar

Type 24 fortunes on thin strips of paper. Preheat oven to 350°. Put all ingredients in food processor & blend 10~15 seconds. Cover cookie sheets with parchment paper, then grease the paper. Do only four at a time, dropping by measured tablespoonfuls on cookie sheet. Bake 10 min. Immediately remove with spatula. The rough side should be on the inside of the cookie. Put the fortune in the middle of the cookie, fold it in half — bring corners up. Let oven cool completely to 200°. Put all the finished cookies back on cookie sheet & bake till completely browned, about ½ hr. Put one in the toe of each Christmas stocking, serve them at birthdays, send them in the mail; feel free to predict the future. ♥

This person deserves more than fortune cookies for dessert — A surprise in the freezer!

POTATO SKINS WITH DIP

450° Serves Six

Who doesn't like potato skins? This is a very special dip & also tastes great with cold Roasted Green Beans (p.72). ♥

12 baking potatoes
5 green onions, chopped
1 clove garlic
½ c. parsley, chopped

3/4 c. mayonnaise
½ c. sour cream
1½ tsp. Worcestershire
3 drops Tabasco

Preheat oven to 450°. With a sharp knife, peel the potatoes lengthwise, taking a bit of potato with the skin, into 1" strips. (Save potatoes for salad or whatever.) Put the strips, skin side up, on a buttered cookie sheet. Bake 20 min. till golden; remove from oven, salt lightly & cool. Put all remaining ingredients into food processor or blender & mix till smooth. Cover & chill. Serve with potato skins at room temperature. ♥

"I never see any home cooking. All I get is fancy stuff."
Duke of Edinburgh

SALSA

Makes 2+ cups

Fresh homemade salsa is a far cry from most of the canned or bottled versions I've tasted. Serve it, along with a bowl of sour cream, as a dip for tortilla chips, as a topping for tacos, or with Quesadillas (p.116). ♥

3 lg. vine-ripened summer tomatoes, squeezed and finely chopped
3/4 c. green onions, chopped
3 Tbsp. green chilies, minced
    (use jalapeño if you want it hot)
1 Tbsp. cilantro, minced
½ tsp. celery seed
1 Tbsp. red wine vinegar
salt & freshly ground black pepper, to taste

Cut the tomatoes in half & squeeze the insides into a bowl. Finely chop them & add to the bowl with all other ingredients. Chill well before serving ♥.

"The right food always comes at the right time. Reliance on out-of-season foods makes the gastronomic year an endlessly boring repetition."
♥ Roy Andries De Groot

STUFFED EGGS

These are always a nice thing to serve along with all the "foo—foo" hors d'oeuvres — the men love them, they're substantial & there's never any left over.

hard-boiled eggs

sweet pickle relish

celery seed

freshly ground pepper

minced celery

dash Tabasco

mayonnaise

sweet pickle juice

Peel the hard-boiled eggs. (The fresher they are, the harder to peel.) Cut them in half lengthwise. Remove yolks to bowl. Put whites on serving dish. Mash yolks with potato masher & stir in all other ingredients (except pickle juice) to taste. If you need to thin it or if you like it sweeter, use the pickle juice (from the relish jar). Don't go overboard on the mayonnaise — it makes them boring. Taste as you go — pile yolk mixture back into whites. Refrigerate till time to serve. ♥

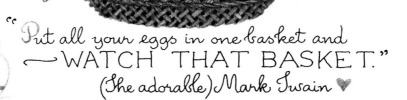

"Put all your eggs in one basket and — WATCH THAT BASKET."
(The adorable) Mark Twain ♥

ESCARGOTS
450° Makes 1½ dozen

The perfect start for a French meal. Make sure you have some good French bread for mopping up the garlic butter. Shells & canned snails are available at gourmet food stores. For those that are alarmed at the idea of eating a snail, use a bite~sized piece of cooked sausage to fill the shell, but the truth is—the snails taste best! ♥

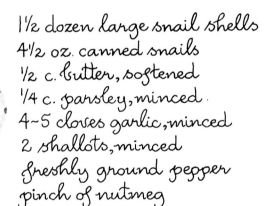

1½ dozen large snail shells
4½ oz. canned snails
½ c. butter, softened
¼ c. parsley, minced
4~5 cloves garlic, minced
2 shallots, minced
freshly ground pepper
pinch of nutmeg

Preheat oven to 450°. Rinse & drain shells; drain snails. Cream together all other ingredients. Put a snail in each shell, then fill to top with butter mixture. Heat them in the oven till bubbling hot. Serve with French bread ♥. Handy to have: metal snail dishes to balance the shells as they cook & some little 2-pronged forks to eat them with. ♥

SQUID

Serves Six

For those of us who still get flashbacks from the movie "20,000 Leagues Under the Sea," it's very hard to imagine EATING a squid. But they're light, chewy & <u>delicious</u>.

2 lbs. fresh squid, cleaned
flour for dredging
oil for frying
Garlic Tartar Sauce

Make the Tartar Sauce, cover & refrigerate. Rinse the squid (your fish-person will clean it). Slice the fish into ¼" to ½" strips; pat dry with paper towels; dredge in flour. Fry quickly, a few at a time, in ½" very hot oil. Drain on paper towels. Serve warm with

Garlic Tartar Sauce

1½ c. mayonnaise	1½ Tbsp. green onion, minced
2 cloves garlic, minced	2 Tbsp. capers
2 Tbsp. parsley, minced	1 Tbsp. sweet pickle, minced
	2½ Tbsp. cider vinegar

Mix all ingredients & refrigerate. ♥

BACON & CREAM-CHEESE TOMATOES
Makes about 50

about 3 pints cherry tomatoes, tops  removed
2 8-oz. pkg. cream cheese, softened
12 slices bacon, crisply cooked & drained on paper towels
¼ c. green onions, minced
¼ c. parsley, minced
½ tsp. Worcestershire sauce

Hollow out cherry tomatoes with melon baller. Beat
together cream cheese, crumbled bacon, onions, parsley
& Worcestershire sauce. Stuff mixture into tomatoes. ♥

GARLIC & HERB POPCORN
Makes 1 big bowlful

⅓ c. popping corn
2 Tbsp. oil
⅓ c. butter
3 cloves garlic, minced
1 tsp. dry dillweed or thyme

Pop the popcorn in a big (3 qt.) pot in the 2 Tbsp. oil.
Meanwhile, melt butter, add garlic & cook 1-2 min.
Stir in dill; pour over popcorn & toss. ♥

"Beware of all enterprises that require new
clothes." ♥ Henry David Thoreau

THE DO-IT-YOURSELF ALL-APPETIZER PARTY

It had been a good week at the old Branch homestead. Suddenly, unexpectedly, we had 6 hungry people in the house. We were sitting there eating this delicious variety of part leftovers, part spur-of-the-moment cooking, when it came to me that I ought to write it all down, mostly because it was being devoured with such obvious relish! It wasn't fancy or elegant but it was fun to watch how creative people could be with such an assortment ~ what they'd put with what ~ it was "oooo, try THIS!" It was spur of the moment — one of those lucky days when there's a ton of stuff in the refrigerator, but I'd even take the time to plan the exact same thing, that's why I wrote it down. ♥ So here's the "menu":

mustard, hot, & sweet
thin slices of rare steak
bermuda onion slices
pickles
smoked bluefish paté
French bread & crackers
apple slices
meat patés, country & smooth
celery stalks

cream cheese
smoked salmon
lemon & lime slices
roasted garlic }see p.12
Montrachet }
jar of sun-dried
 tomatoes
steamed shrimp & sauce
salt & pepper

This, plus some wine & beer & a quick Chocolate Fondue (p.13), is a feast! Try it instead of a sit-down dinner ~ have all appetizers & eat in the kitchen. ♥

CHEESE

When you're too busy to cook, you can have very elegant hors d'oeuvres direct from your gourmet food store. They allow tasting; pick up your favorite cheese, a slice of beautiful paté, some gherkins & Greek olives ~ slice an apple & voilà: food! Here are some cheeses & ideas:

KASSERI: This cheese makes a delicious snack called "saganaki". Sauté slices in frying pan with a little butter Serve sizzling hot with fresh lemon juice & pita or French bread. ♥

PARMIGIANO-REGGIANO: The very best Parmesan ~ from Italy. ♥

MONTRACHET: My favorite goat cheese (chevre). Best when very fresh ~ it's moist & creamy. Sometimes in olive oil with thyme; delicious baked (see pg.12) or broken over lettuce leaves, peppered & tossed with balsamic vinegar. ♥

EXPLORATEUR: Very rich ~ a triple cream cheese like St. Andre. Creamy & spreadable; it needs to be fresh. ♥

PORT SALUT: Semi-soft & smooth. The best has S.A.F.R. stamped on rind. Good with fruit ~ mild. ♥

FETA: There are lots of different ones ~ the creamier, milder ones come from Germany or Bulgaria. Good in salads. ♥

STILTON: This is an English cheese, a combination of cheddar & blue, so it has a little tang. ♥

MASCARPONE: From Italy, fresh, delicate, buttery. Good with fruit ~ pears & strawberries, ♥ especially.

31

SPRING

"Not a creature was stirring, not even a mouse" certainly fits for the quiet winter but in spring the creatures start stirring like mad. In April I start going out daily to see what's new. I lift some of the winter mulch to see the green shoots of the new plants — the mint is more than a survivor — I think it might be a predator! I even find it growing under the remains of the last snow. Spring is heard as much as seen — the birds & creatures are all so busy starting their families. It's time to air the quilts, think about the gardens, take off the storm windows, go for long walks & buy a new hat. It passes so quickly & in no time at all it's time to mow the first grass — what a wonderful smell that is. I think the island must look like a carpet of yellow from the air when the daffodils are in bloom. Spring is magic — sweet to the senses & easy to celebrate.

"May Day" is a charming custom that seems to have slipped in popularity, but when I was a child we used to make baskets out of woven strips of construction paper, tied with ribbons & filled with sugar cookies & with all the flowers we could find, both wild & not so wild (ahem!). Sometimes we'd make cornucopias out of old flowered wallpaper. On May 1st we'd place them on the front porches of favorite friends, ring the doorbell & run like crazy to hide & watch the surprise. I'm not sure who felt best, our friends — or us!

MORE  SPRING

✿ Use pink & yellow & green satin ribbons to tie around napkins, champagne glasses, invitations — makes a pretty table for Easter dinner. Paint names on colored eggs to use for placecards.

✿ Pack a picnic & take your family on a trip to the country. Visit a farm to see all the newborn baby animals.

✿ Air your blankets & quilts on a line in the yard, beat your rugs — take down heavy curtains & replace with something light & fluttery.

✿ Make a new bed in spring. Start with a thick mattress pad & some soft feather pillows — use fresh flowered sheets, a cotton comforter, a lace bed skirt. Open ♥ a nearby window to let in the sounds & smells of spring.

✿ Wild violets are one of the first spring flowers — they grow profusely & make the prettiest of small bouquets. For Mother's Day gather a corsage of violets, tie with a narrow satin ribbon, serve with hat pin to your mom.

✿ Plant radishes & let your children help. They are so easy & so quick that they are almost instant gratification & a good way to start young gardeners. Serve them sliced on buttered French bread, well salted & peppered.

✿ Make "sun tea" — put 5 tea bags in a half-gallon glass jar, fill with cold water & set it outside in the sun to steep. Serve it iced with lemon, sugar, & mint sprigs.

✿ Fly an American flag on Flag Day & Memorial Day. Get a tiny one for your car antenna for the trip to the Memorial Day picnic. ♥ It's spring, so sing ♪!

A Gift of Garlic

A wonderful, inexpensive gift for your friends — especially if you grow your own garlic. ♥ Just peel the cloves, put them in a jar, pour olive oil over just to cover, & seal jar. They keep for weeks in the refrigerator & it's so nice to have a supply of ready-to-use garlic & the added bonus of the garlic-flavored olive oil ♥.

SALADS

ICED SCALLOP SALAD

Serves Four

An elegant first course ~ for a light summer dinner include Lemon Noodles (p. 98), Roasted Green Beans (p. 72), & sautéed cherry tomatoes.

1 lb. scallops
juice of 1 juicy lime
1/4 c. watercress leaves
1/2 c. mayonnaise
2 Tbsp. green onion

2 Tbsp. parsley
1 tsp. fresh dill
2 tsp. lime juice
mixed salad greens

If you can't find the tiny Bay scallops, use the larger Sea scallops & cut them into bite~sized pieces. Rinse & drain them. Steam them in water just until done (don't overcook!). Drain, squeeze over lime juice, cover & chill. Put remaining ingredients (except greens) into food processor & process till smooth. Refrigerate. To serve: arrange greens on salad plates, divide scallops among them & top with a dollop of the lovely green sauce. ♥

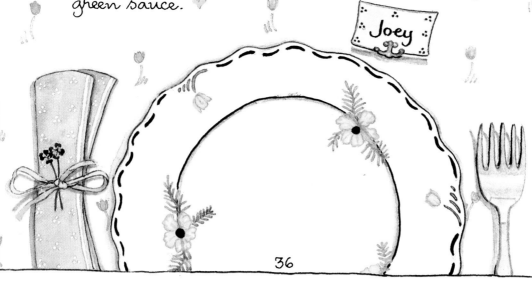

COLE•SLAW

Serves Six

Bright, fresh & crisp. Serve a big bowl of this colorful salad for a picnic or barbecue. ♥

2 c. red cabbage, thinly shredded
2 c. green cabbage, thinly shredded
1 c. grated carrots
1 Tbsp. grated onion
¼ c. cider vinegar
¼ c. salad oil
1 Tbsp. brown sugar
¼ tsp. salt
freshly ground black pepper

Combine shredded cabbages, carrots, & onion in a large bowl. Whisk together vinegar, oil, brown sugar, salt, & pepper. Pour over salad & toss. Serve chilled. ♥

"Ten years ago the deficit on my farm was about a hundred dollars; but by well-designed capital expenditure, by drainage and by greater attention to details, I have got it into the thousands."
Stephen Leacock

FRESH FLOWER SALAD
With Vinaigrette

All of these flowers are easy to grow & they
make a really pretty summer salad. Start
a small salad garden of your own — grow
leaf lettuce, garlic, chives, herbs, & flowers.
That way you'll have everything perfectly fresh
and unsprayed. The fresh flowers are becoming
available in supermarkets & health food stores. ♥

violets & pansies in all colors
Johnny-jump-ups
nasturtiums, all colors
roses, wild or cultivated, petals only
forget-me-nots
parsley heads
curly-leafed endive
red lettuce (Salad Bowl)

Pick the flowers early in the   day & refrigerate.
They bruise easily so handle   carefully. Put the
lettuce in a salad bowl,   add the parsley
(stemmed & in chunks, not   chopped). Dress
& toss with Vinaigrette; strew   flowers over & serve. ♥

Vinaigrette

minced garlic, mustard, pepper   Mix the garlic, etc., with
1 part balsamic vinegar   the vinegar. Beat in oil
3 parts olive oil   slowly. Add a little
light cream   cream, mix well. ♥

38

FARMER SALAD

Serves Four

1 c. sour cream or yogurt
1 c. cottage cheese
4 green onions, minced
10 radishes, sliced
1 cucumber, chopped
½ tsp. dill
½ tsp. celery seed
freshly ground pepper

Mix all ingredients. Chill. Serve on a bed of fresh greens. ♥

CRANBERRY SAUCE

Makes 3 Cups

A Thanksgiving tradition 🍂. I always receive compliments for this recipe. ♥ For a pretty, seasonal decoration, buy an extra pound of fresh cranberries; put them in an old wooden bowl or basket to set out for holiday color 🌲.

1 lb. fresh cranberries	3/4 c. sugar
1 apple, peeled, cored & chopped	1/2 c. water
2 lg. oranges, peeled & chopped	juice of 1 juicy lemon

Combine all ingredients in a heavy saucepan. Cover & cook over very low heat, stirring occasionally, for 3 or 4 hours. Serve hot or cold. Also good on sandwiches with turkey and stuffing. ♥

"I love everything that's old: old friends, old times, old manners, old books, old wines."
♥ Oliver Goldsmith

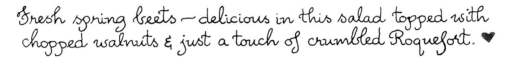

BEET
SALAD

Serves Six

Fresh spring beets — delicious in this salad topped with chopped walnuts & just a touch of crumbled Roquefort. ♥

5 medium beets
4 Tbsp. red wine vinegar
2 Tbsp. salad oil
1 small red onion, sliced

½ c. sour cream
½ c. chopped walnuts
Roquefort cheese, to taste
Freshly ground pepper

Wash & trim beets. Cook in boiling water till tender. Drain & cool; peel them, cut into julienne strips. Put into bowl with thinly sliced onion & toss with vinegar & oil. Add the sour cream & mix gently. Sprinkle on walnuts, crumble on cheese & grind pepper over. Serve on a bed of torn salad greens if you like. ♥

SUMMER SALAD WITH ROSEMARY

Serves Four

Rosemary grows like a fiend, makes a wonderful ground cover, deters garden pests, & tastes like heaven in this delicious salad. ♡ Your local gourmet food store should be able to supply anything your regular market doesn't carry. ♥

½ lb. orzo pasta
1½ c. pine nuts, toasted
1 c. Montrachet or feta cheese
1 or 2 cloves garlic, minced

¼ c. fresh rosemary
¼ c. olive oil
juice from 1 lemon
1 c. Niçoise olives

Orzo is a tiny rice-like pasta, available in super-markets. Cook the orzo in boiling water, careful not to overcook; drain, rinse in cold water. Lightly brown pine nuts in butter; set aside to cool. Crumble (in big bits) the cheese over the pasta. Mince the garlic & rosemary & lightly toss all ingredients together except the olives. Refrigerate till ready to serve; then either put a few olives on each serving plate, or surround the salad bowl with them.

"There's rosemary, that's for remembrance; pray, love, remember..." ♥ Wm. Shakespeare

FRESH APPLESAUCE

Serves Four

Because it's not cooked, this applesauce has a wonderful fresh flavor — great for your kids. The frozen banana makes it icy cold, & you can blend it to the consistency you like, chunky or smooth. ♥

1 frozen banana
3 lg. green apples
1/4 tsp. each cinnamon & nutmeg
1/2 c. apple juice

Peel, slice, wrap & freeze the banana. Peel the apples, set one aside, core & chop the other two. Put the frozen banana, the two chopped apples, cinnamon, nutmeg & juice into blender or food processor — blend till smooth. Remove to bowl & grate in the other apple. Stir & serve. ♥

"I have always maintained that there is nothing wrong with nursery food now that we are grown up and can have a glass of wine with it."
♥ Elizabeth Ray

PINE NUT SALAD

Serves Six

When it's your turn to bring the salad, bring this one! Served cold, it's fresh, flavorful & fun. *Yes*

2 c. pine nuts
2 Tbsp. butter
½ lb. alphabet pasta
1 c. black olives, sliced
½ c. parsley, minced
½ c. green onion, minced

⅓ c. green bell pepper
⅓ c. red bell pepper
¼ c. fresh lemon juice
¼ c. olive oil
Freshly ground pepper
Parmesan cheese, to taste

In a large skillet, lightly toast the pine nuts in the butter; drain on paper towels & cool. Cook the alphabet pasta in boiling water; drain & rinse in cold water. (Be extra careful not to overcook the pasta.) Very gently, mix together all ingredients; cover & chill. *Brrr*

"Little Willie from his mirror
Licked the mercury right off,
Thinking in his childish error,
It would cure the whooping cough.
At the funeral his mother
Smartly said to Mrs. Brown:
"Twas a chilly day for Willie
When the mercury went down.""
♥ Anonymous

RASPBERRIES & WATERCRESS

Serves Four

Beautiful in summer. ♥

1¼ c. fresh raspberries
¼ c. walnut or olive oil
grated rind of 1 orange
¼ c. fresh orange juice
3 tbsp. raspberry vinegar
1 tsp. honey
freshly ground pepper
1 c. walnuts, coarsely chopped & toasted
4 c. fresh watercress, tough stems removed
thinly sliced red onion

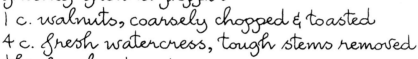

Force ¼ c. raspberries through a sieve & into shaker jar; add next six ingredients & shake well. Spread walnuts on cookie sheet & bake in 350° oven 5 min. until toasted. Toss together remaining raspberries, watercress, walnuts & red onion. Dress & serve. ♥

"Thou shalt sit on a cushion and sew a fine seam and feed upon strawberries, sugar and cream." ♥
Anonymous

BUTTER LETTUCE SALAD

Serves Four

Soft lettuce, sun-dried tomatoes & fresh mushrooms
in a hot dressing — a great beginning to any
special meal — delicious with Sole Meunière (p.113).

½ c. sun-dried tomatoes in oil
olive oil, if needed
4 c. torn butter lettuce leaves
1 c. sliced mushrooms
¼ c. red wine vinegar
freshly ground pepper

Drain tomatoes; reserve oil & add enough olive oil
(if necessary) to equal ½ cup. Sliver tomatoes & mix
with lettuce. In a skillet, combine mushrooms
with the oil; stir over high heat till hot; add
vinegar, & pepper to taste. Pour over salad & toss
lightly. Serve. ♡

♥ ♥ ♥ ♥ ♥

"I have been here before,
But when or how I cannot tell;
I know the grass beyond the door,
The sweet keen smell,
The sighing sound, the lights around the
   shore."   ♡ Dante Gabriel Rossetti

GREEK POTATO SALAD

Serves Eight

I love any kind of potato salad but this one is especially good with the tart bits of Greek olives. ♥

2 lb. med. red potatoes
2/3 c. olive oil
1/3 c. red wine vinegar
1/2 tsp. oregano
1/2 tsp. rosemary, crumbled
1/2 lb. feta cheese, crumbled
1 sweet red pepper, seeded & chopped
1/2 c. green onion, chopped
1/2 c. Kalamata olives, pitted & chopped
salt & freshly ground pepper, to taste

Cook the potatoes in boiling water, jackets on, till tender. Drain thoroughly & put into lg. salad bowl. Coarsely cut them into bite-sized pieces. Mix together oil, vinegar, oregano, & rosemary; pour over potatoes. Add remaining ingredients; toss gently. Let stand 1/2 hr. so flavors marry. Serve at room temperature. ♥

"In all things of nature there is something of the marvelous." ♥
Aristotle

CHEVRE SALAD

My favorite summer salad. The vinegar mixes with the cheese & makes a delicious fresh dressing; no oil! We take it to the beach in a covered bowl with 2 forks.
Toss together to taste:
soft lettuce, butter or Bibb
Montrachet cheese, crumbled
freshly ground pepper
Balsamic vinegar
cooked chicken, opt.

VELVET CHICKEN SALAD

Serves Four to Six

2 whole boned & skinned
   chicken breasts
4 Tbsp. cornstarch
2 egg whites
½ tsp. salt
2 tsp. light soy sauce
ice water
½ lb. snow peas
1 Tbsp. fresh ginger, minced

3 cloves garlic, minced
¼ c. toasted sesame seeds
¼ c. fresh lemon juice
¼ c. salad oil
1 Tbsp. light soy sauce
1 8½-oz. can pineapple
   chunks, drained
1 8-oz. can sliced water
   chestnuts, drained

Cut chicken in bite-sized pieces. In a med. bowl mix together cornstarch & egg whites; stir in chicken. In a saucepan, bring 3 qts. water, salt & soy sauce to a boil. Fill a large bowl with ice & water & set aside. Set a colander in the sink. Add chicken to boiling water — as soon as it comes back to the boil, remove from heat & let stand 1 minute. Drain in colander & immediately plunge chicken into ice water. Let it sit for 2 minutes; drain & put into salad bowl. Blanch snow peas in boiling water 1 min.; drain, rinse in cold water & add to salad bowl along with all other ingredients.

"The carp was dead, killed, assassinated, murdered in the first, second and third degree. Limp, I fell into a chair, with my hands still unwashed reached for a cigarette, lighted it, and waited for the police to come take me into custody." ♥ Alice B. Toklas

ORANGE & ONION

Ice-cold oranges, crisp red onion — make the perfect salad for Christmas dinner.

Per Person :
> 1 navel orange, peeled & sliced
> 1 slice red onion, in rings
> ½ Tbsp. olive oil
> a squeeze of fresh lime juice
> a grating of fresh black pepper

When you peel the oranges they should be cold & you should use a knife — make sure you remove all the white stuff from the outside of the orange. Arrange orange slices & onion rings on salad plates. Sprinkle olive oil & lime juice over them; grind on pepper. Serve chilled. ♥

"Most all the time, the whole year
round, there ain't no flies on me,
But jest 'fore Christmas
I'm as good as I kin be!"
                    Eugene Field

TWO GREAT SALAD DRESSINGS

Cream 'n' Bacon

Makes 1 cup

6 slices bacon
1 Tbsp. olive oil
1/3 c. shallots, minced
1/3 c. red wine vinegar
3/4 c. heavy cream
freshly ground pepper

Fry the bacon crisp, remove and set aside. Pour out all but 1 Tbsp. bacon grease, add 1 Tbsp. olive oil & sauté shallots slowly till soft & golden. Scrape up any bits of bacon stuck to pan. Stir in vinegar, then cream. Mix well, heat through but don't boil. Crumble bacon over crisp cold greens & pour hot dressing over. Serve. 🌿 Can be reheated. ♥

Spicy Herb

Makes 1 1/4 cups

1/2 c. mayonnaise
1/2 c. sour cream
2 tsp. anchovy paste
2 Tbsp. tarragon vinegar

1 green onion
1 clove garlic
3/4 c. parsley
1 Tbsp. fresh basil

Put all ingredients into blender or food processor & blend till smooth. Cover & chill ♥

SUMMERTIME

In the summer the fireflies come out ~ they blink like a million tiny lights in the woods. I feel like they must be some sort of legacy from Walt Disney, master of the tiny light. Summer magic is everywhere on Martha's Vineyard. Sometimes it is so beautiful that as I walk or drive around it seems as if there are fairies running ahead to set up scenes just for my plea-sure. ♥ Gardens go wild: the corn begins to ripen, the tomatoes turn red & sweet, the perennial garden is thick with summer bloom (the weeds go berserk, the lawn grows WAY too fast). ♥ There are picnics, outdoor concerts, & cookouts; beach trips, country fairs & jam making & there seems to be a rush for enjoyment ~ it all ends so soon. Summer dreams, summer schemes: Take a day a month to visit local art galleries ~ there are special openings in the summer; they usually have wine & appetizers & some beautiful art. ♥ Early on summer mornings go to yard sales. Collect old creamers & sugar bowls for your flowers & plants. ♥ Wonderful: screened porches, unscreened porches, glassed porches & unglassed ~ with old wicker chairs, pots of geraniums ~ all bring romance to summer. ♥

...Summer Dreams & Schemes:

For the table: take tiny seashells & fill them with wet sand; poke in the stems of little flowers ~ one for each place setting. ♥

Plan a hot summer midnight supper on the beach or near a lake ~ a real expedition. Bring candles, music, blankets, pillows, champagne & cold oysters; chocolate truffles, St. Andre cheese & cold lobster meat. Enjoy a summer moon. ♥

Take your family berry picking ~ take baskets & buckets & get those berries. Make jam & berry pies.

Set an old chair or wicker rocker out in the garden. ♥

On a hot, hot day when everyone is quick to argue or too lazy to move ~ go get some root beer & some ice cream ~ make big root beer floats with long spoons & straws. Wash the car; be liberal with the hose. ♥

Pick a flower here and there ~ put them between the pages of a big heavy book to dry. Use them in cards & letters come winter. ♥

Shine up your indoor plants ~ wash the leaves with water & then rub each one with a tiny bit of mayonnaise. It doesn't hurt them a bit. ♥

"Summer afternoon ~ summer afternoon;
to me those have always been the two most
beautiful words in the English language." ♥
Henry James

"Strephon kissed me in the spring,
Robin in the fall,
But Colin only looked at me
And never kissed at all.
Strephon's kiss was lost in jest,
Robin's lost in play,
But the kiss in Colin's eyes
Haunts me night and day."
    ♥ Sara Teasdale

"There is a garden in her face
Where roses and white lilies grow."
    ♥ Thomas Campion

VEGETABLES

" Earth is here so kind, that just tickle
her with a hoe and she laughs with a
harvest." ♥ Douglas Jerrold

GARLIC &
POTATOES

350° Serves Two

Roasted, the garlic becomes mellow & sweet, the potatoes take on the flavors of garlic and thyme. For a picnic or barbecue they can be made in individual foil packages. ♥

♥ Double or triple this recipe to serve more:
6~7 small red potatoes, quartered
10 whole large cloves garlic, unpeeled
2 Tbsp. good olive oil
sprinkle of thyme, or fresh thyme branches
1 Tbsp. white wine
good grinding of fresh black pepper
sprinkle of salt

Preheat oven to 350°. Put all ingredients into baking dish; dribble over olive oil & wine. Cover tightly with foil & bake 1 hour. Serve. (The garlic will slip right out of the skin — don't eat the skin. ☺) ♥

"From the dog's point of view his master is an elongated and abnormally cunning dog."

♥ Mabel Robinson

"JACK BE LITTLE" TINY PUMPKINS

350°

We had a Halloween dinner last year & started with a tiny pumpkin on each plate — it was the perfect beginning! They would also look (and taste) great for Thanksgiving.

1 miniature pumpkin per person
1 Tbsp. butter (each)
1 tsp. brown sugar
sprinkle of cinnamon & nutmeg

Preheat oven to 350°. Cut off the very top of each pumpkin — about a quarter of the way down. Scoop out the seeds & strings. Put butter, brown sugar, cinnamon & nutmeg in each pumpkin — put the tops back on. Place them on a cookie sheet & bake 45 ~ 55 min., till fork-tender. Serve.

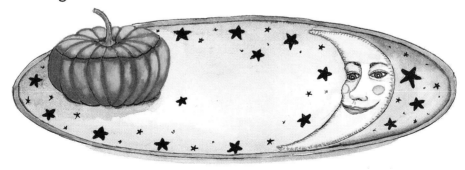

The official name for these pumpkins is "Jack Be Little Mini Pumpkins."

APPLE & SWEET POTATO PURÉE

350° Serves Six

Serve this in late Fall with pork or chicken, at breakfast with sausage or bacon, or to your children for a healthy after-school tummy warmer.

2 medium sweet potatoes
6 Tbsp. unsalted butter
6 tart apples (Granny Smith), peeled, cored & sliced
½ tsp. cinnamon
1 Tbsp. fresh lemon juice
½ c. walnuts, chopped (opt.)

Bake the potatoes at 350° for 1 hour, till fork-tender. Cool to handle; cut in half, remove pulp, discard skins. In a large skillet, over med. heat, melt 1 Tbsp. of the butter. Add the apple slices; cover & cook for about 10-15 min., till soft & mushy. Put the apples, potato pulp, remaining butter, cinnamon & lemon juice in food processor & process till smooth. Serve hot with a sprinkle of walnuts, if desired. ♥ To reheat, put a little apple juice in a saucepan & heat slowly over low flame. ♥

"Part of the secret of success in life is to eat what you like and let the food fight it out inside." ♥ Mark Twain

58

SUMMER TOMATOES

Serves Four

My grandma used to make this for us with the wonderful fresh tomatoes from her garden. Don't bother with it unless you have the firm, vine-ripened tomatoes of summer. ♥

3 Tbsp. butter
1 med. onion, minced
4 good tomatoes, halved

2 Tbsp. basil, minced
2/3 c. heavy cream
fresh pepper

Sauté the onions slowly in the butter till soft & golden. Put the tomatoes in the pan, cut side down, & sauté 5~7 min. Pierce skin with fork, turn them, sprinkle with basil. Cook 5 more min. Pour cream around tomatoes & boil. Add pepper to taste. Spoon sauce onto plates, set tomato in center & serve. ♥

59

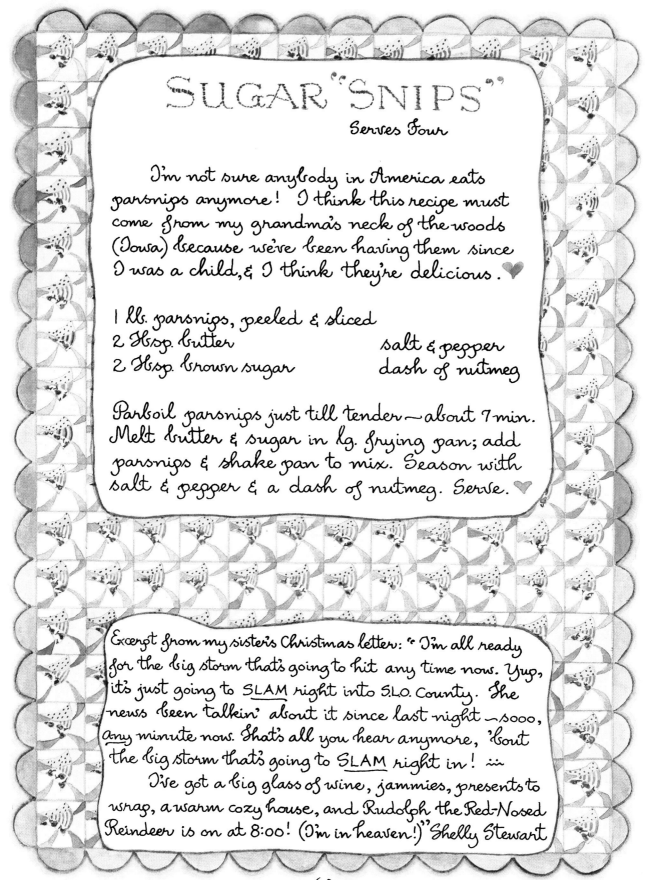

SUGAR "SNIPS"

Serves Four

I'm not sure anybody in America eats parsnips anymore! I think this recipe must come from my grandma's neck of the woods (Iowa) because we've been having them since I was a child, & I think they're delicious. ♥

1 lb. parsnips, peeled & sliced
2 Tbsp. butter
2 Tbsp. brown sugar

salt & pepper
dash of nutmeg

Parboil parsnips just till tender — about 7 min. Melt butter & sugar in lg. frying pan; add parsnips & shake pan to mix. Season with salt & pepper & a dash of nutmeg. Serve. ♥

Excerpt from my sister's Christmas letter: "I'm all ready for the big storm that's going to hit any time now. Yup, it's just going to SLAM right into S.L.O. County. The news been talkin' about it since last night — sooo, any minute now. That's all you hear anymore, 'bout the big storm that's going to SLAM right in! ⋯
I've got a big glass of wine, jammies, presents to wrap, a warm cozy house, and Rudolph the Red-Nosed Reindeer is on at 8:00! (I'm in heaven!)" Shelly Stewart

ASPARAGUS
in Mustard Cream Sauce
Serves Four

I finally planted asparagus. I was put off originally by the knowledge that I'd have to wait 2 years for my first harvest — but those 2 years, needless to say, passed anyway & my asparagus bed is now one of my garden "jewels." Every spring now, the tender spears come up to help us celebrate the season. Well worth the "wait."

¼ c. good dry white wine
½ c. heavy cream
1 tsp. Dijon mustard
3 Tbsp. butter
1½ lbs. fresh asparagus

In a medium skillet, boil wine, heavy cream & mustard till reduced by half, stirring constantly. Stir in butter until melted; keep over low heat while you steam the asparagus till tender—crisp. Arrange asparagus & pour sauce over. Serve. ♥

"The strongest of all warriors are these two
— Time and Patience."
Leo Tolstoi

SUCCOTASH

Serves Four to Six

This is an old favorite; nice texture between the corn & beans, sweetened with tomatoes & cream ♥. You could use fresh corn off the cob, fresh garden tomatoes & long cooked beans — it's wonderful that way. But, here I'm giving you the faster "winter version" — you can always have the ingredients on hand, & this delicious dish all year long ♥.

  1 9~oz. pkg. frozen baby lima beans
  1 10~oz. pkg. frozen corn
  2 14~oz. cans whole tomatoes (2 c. fresh, peeled
      and chopped)
  4 Tbsp. butter
  ⅓ c. heavy cream
  salt & freshly ground pepper, to taste

Cook the lima beans in boiling water 10 min. Add corn & cook 3 min. longer, drain. Drain the tomatoes. Melt butter in large skillet; add corn, beans, & tomatoes — stir, breaking the tomatoes up with the spoon. Stir in cream & salt & pepper. Heat through and serve ♥

"Don't part with your illusions. When they are gone, you may still exist, but you have ceased to live." ♥ Mark Twain

62

SPINACH & HEARTS

350° Serves Six

The _perfect_ vegetable for Valentine's!

2 red bell peppers
2 pkg. frozen chopped
   spinach, thawed
1 Tbsp. butter
1/3 c. shallots, minced
3/4 c. Swiss cheese, grated
1 Tbsp. Romano cheese

1/2 c. fresh breadcrumbs
1/4 tsp. nutmeg
4 beaten eggs
1/4 c. milk
1/2 c. heavy cream
Freshly ground pepper,
   to taste

Cut out 6 1-inch hearts from the peppers. Thaw, drain,
& squeeze the spinach. Preheat oven to 350° & oil 6 custard
cups. Put a heart into the bottom of each cup, skin
down. Put butter & shallots into skillet~cook slowly
till tender. Put into large bowl with cheeses, crumbs &
nutmeg; add beaten eggs; mix well. Slightly warm the
milk & cream & beat into egg mixture; stir in spinach,
add pepper. Pour into cups. Put them into lg. pan;
place pan in lower part of oven & add 1 1/2 in. hot water to pan. Bake 40 min., till knife comes out clean.
Cool, out of water, for a few minutes. Cut tightly
around sides with sharp knife. Invert onto plates. ♥

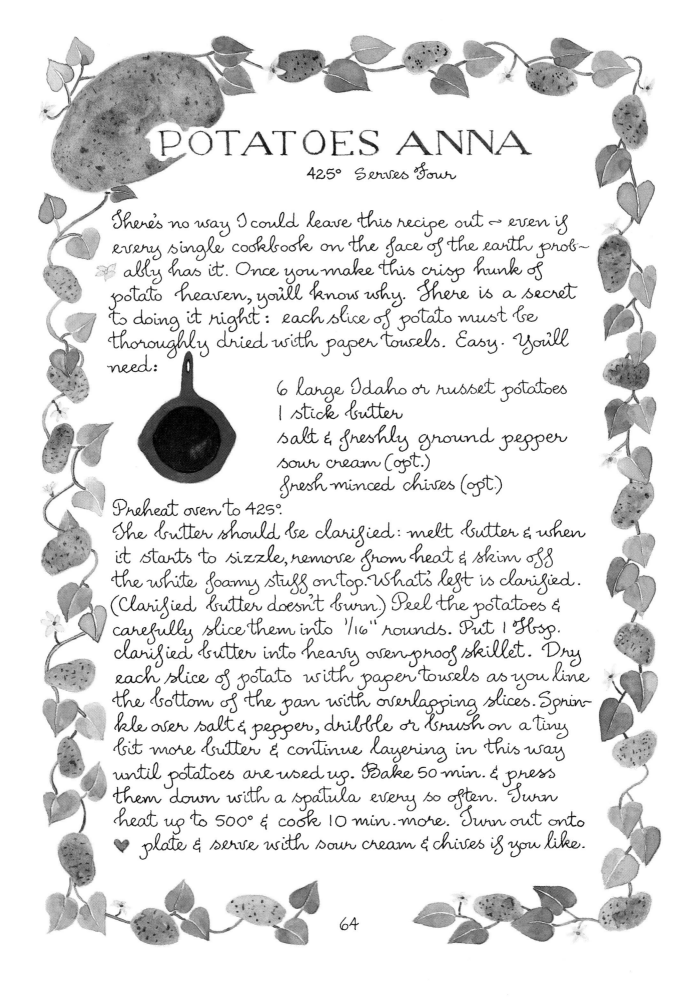

POTATOES ANNA
425° Serves Four

There's no way I could leave this recipe out ~ even if every single cookbook on the face of the earth prob~ ably has it. Once you make this crisp hunk of potato heaven, you'll know why. There is a secret to doing it right: each slice of potato must be thoroughly dried with paper towels. Easy. You'll need:

6 large Idaho or russet potatoes
1 stick butter
salt & freshly ground pepper
sour cream (opt.)
fresh minced chives (opt.)

Preheat oven to 425°.
The butter should be clarified: melt butter & when it starts to sizzle, remove from heat & skim off the white foamy stuff on top. What's left is clarified. (Clarified butter doesn't burn.) Peel the potatoes & carefully slice them into 1/16" rounds. Put 1 Tbsp. clarified butter into heavy oven-proof skillet. Dry each slice of potato with paper towels as you line the bottom of the pan with overlapping slices. Sprin~ kle over salt & pepper, dribble or brush on a tiny bit more butter & continue layering in this way until potatoes are used up. Bake 50 min. & press them down with a spatula every so often. Turn heat up to 500° & cook 10 min. more. Turn out onto plate & serve with sour cream & chives if you like.

MUSHROOM PANCAKES
Serves Four

Crisp little critters; delicious served with a little sour cream.

2 c. minced mushrooms
2 eggs, beaten
1 c. grated cheddar cheese
1/4 c. minced green onions
1/2 c. unbleached flour

1/2 tsp. baking powder
1/2 tsp. salt
1/4 tsp. thyme
1 Tbsp. oil
sour cream, garnish

Mince mushrooms (in food processor) & wring in towel to remove excess moisture. Beat eggs, add cheese, onions, & mushrooms. Combine dry ingredients & stir into mushroom mixture. Heat oil & drop mixture into skillet by tablespoonfuls. Brown on both sides. Serve with sour cream. ♥

SUMMER CORN

For a very large group at a barbecue, it's nice to serve the corn on the cob this way ~ no fights at the butter dish! ♥

Husk the corn, butter well with softened butter; salt & pepper. Wrap each piece in aluminum foil. Bake in 400° oven for 10~15 min. till heated through. ♥

CABBAGE WITH CARAWAY & BACON
Serves Four

Have this with a pork roast & some ice-cold Cranberry Sauce (pg. 40) for a delicious dinner in winter. ♥

4 slices bacon
½ Tbsp. vegetable oil
4 c. shredded cabbage
1 Tbsp. caraway seeds
2 Tbsp. cider vinegar
salt & freshly ground pepper, to taste

Cook bacon till crisp; drain on paper towels. In a large skillet with a cover, heat oil. Add cabbage, toss to coat with oil. Cover, reduce heat, cook till tender, stirring occasionally (10~15 min.). Sprinkle over caraway seeds, vinegar, & salt & pepper. Toss. Crumble bacon over & serve. ♥

STEAMED SPINACH
Serves Two

It's easy, very healthy, and my favorite. ♥

Wash & stem one large bunch spinach. Put it in a large saucepan with a little water & steam till wilted. Drain. Serve with a splash of cider or balsamic vinegar. Add toasted sesame seeds, if desired.

PEAS & CARROTS COPENHAGEN

Serves Four

I ate this every single day I was in Copenhagen, dissected it & brought it home  Now I serve it at Easter Dinner & every other time I want something special ♥

2 carrots
1 10-oz. pkg. frozen baby peas
½ c. sour cream
1 Tbsp. fresh lemon juice
2 tsp. fresh chives, chopped
1 Tbsp. fresh dill, minced
freshly ground pepper to taste

Cut the carrots into sticks ~ steam till tender & refresh in cold water. Cook & drain peas. Cube carrots into pea-sized pieces. Mix together peas, carrots & all other ingredients. Chill. ♥

"'Mid pleasures and palaces
though we may roam,
Be it ever so humble, there's
no place like Home."
♥ J. Howard Payne

POTATO HEAVEN

Serves One

Do you feel blue? Do you need a hug, a cuddle, a love? Then this is for you, from me, with T.L.C. It's perfect on rainy days & almost cures heartache.

Take about 1½ c. leftover mashed potatoes & form them in a nice firm little pancake. Dip it in flour. Melt butter in a small skillet; put the potato in. Cover & cook slowly till browned; turn, add more butter if necessary, continue cooking till other side is done. (Make hot chocolate while it cooks.) Put the potato on a plate, salt it, pepper it, add another chunk of butter — gather your flannel p.j.'s around you — head for bed.

"My soul is crushed, my spirit sore;
I do not like me anymore.
I cavil, quarrel, grumble, grouse.
I ponder on the narrow house.
I shudder at the thought of men. . .
I'm due to fall in love again."
Dorothy Parker

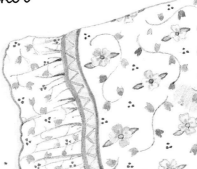

FIDDLEHEAD FERNS

I'm always excited to find something wonderful that I've never tasted before — last spring I found fiddlehead ferns. I'm not sure how available they are in the rest of the country, but I guarantee that very soon they'll be everywhere — they are so delicious. They're easy to grow, a perennial that comes up in my backyard every year with no coaxing. It is the very top of the fern, when it first comes up, all rolled up before it unfurls into fronds. You can steam them & serve with butter & salt & pepper, put them in salads, use them on a crudité plate, stir-fry them. They scream spring — if you find them on a menu or in a market, consider yourself blessed ♥.

"Throw a lucky man into the sea,
and he will come up with a fish
in his mouth."
♥ Arab Proverb

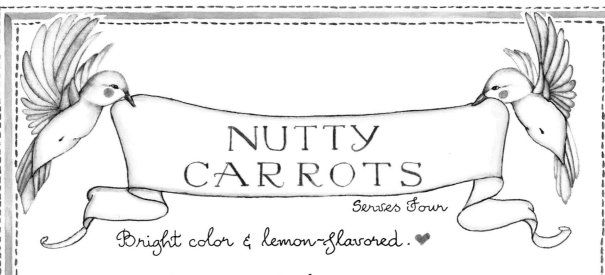

NUTTY CARROTS

Serves Four

Bright color & lemon-flavored. ♥

2/3 c. walnuts, coarsely chopped
4 fresh carrots
2 Tbsp. butter, melted
1/8 tsp. grated lemon peel
1 Tbsp. fresh lemon juice
1 tsp. honey
freshly ground pepper

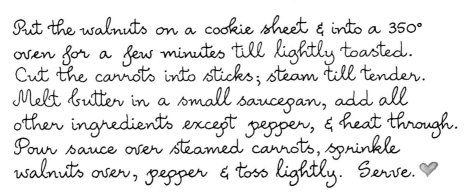

Put the walnuts on a cookie sheet & into a 350°
oven for a few minutes till lightly toasted.
Cut the carrots into sticks; steam till tender.
Melt butter in a small saucepan, add all
other ingredients except pepper, & heat through.
Pour sauce over steamed carrots, sprinkle
walnuts over, pepper & toss lightly. Serve. ♥

"The true way to soften
one's troubles is to solace
those of others." ♥
          Mme. de Maintenon

70

CELERY

I love the flavor of cooked celery — this is an especially easy & delicious side dish.

½ c. slivered almonds
1 Tbsp. butter

3 Tbsp. butter
1 clove garlic, minced
4 c. celery, sliced in thin 1" strips
5 green onions, chopped

Sauté the almonds in 1 Tbsp. butter till light brown. Drain on paper towels & set aside. Melt 3 Tbsp. butter in large skillet. Over low heat, add garlic, celery, & onions; sauté gently, stirring often. Cook until celery is tender—crisp, top with almonds & serve.

If you like cream cheese with your celery & don't mind a few jillion extra calories, try this sauce: melt 6 Tbsp. cream cheese with 6 Tbsp. milk till hot & creamy. Pour over celery & top with toasted almonds.

"Heaven will be no heaven to me if I do not meet my wife there."
Andrew Jackson

ROASTED GREEN BEANS

500° Serves Four

Try these roasted beans cold too — they
make a great hors d'oeuvre when served with
the Dip on p. 24 ♥

1 lb. fresh green beans
1½ Tbsp. olive oil
fresh lemon juice
freshly ground pepper

EXTRA
OLIVE OIL
VIRGIN

SBS

Preheat oven to 500°. Trim the beans, spread
on a cookie sheet, drizzle with oil & bake
for 6~8 min. till tender, turning them
occasionally. Remove to serving dish,
squeeze lemon juice over, pepper & serve.
Good hot or cold. ♥

ZUCCHINI WITH APPLE

Serves Four +

A tasty side dish — we had it last night with the Pasta & Grilled Sausages (p.106) & Fresh Applesauce (p. 43) and it was wonderful for a chilly autumn evening. ♥

½ c. walnut pieces
¼ c. butter
2 small zucchini, grated
1 green apple, peeled & grated
fresh lemon juice
salt & pepper, to taste

Sauté the walnuts in butter over low heat till brown. Take the nuts out of the pan & set aside. Put the grated zucchini in the pan & sauté for 1 minute only. Remove from heat, add walnuts, grated apple & a few drops of lemon juice — stir & taste. Sprinkle on salt & pepper & serve. ♥

" The reader who is illuminated is, in a real sense, the poem." ♥
H. M. Tomlinson

73

FALL

The first time I came to New England, it was Fall & I fell completely in love. ♥ There was a delicious nip in the air as we drove along country roads, the leaves whipping in the wind, through woodland valleys that smelled of the earth, near lakes, brooks & streams all reflecting the flaming colors of the changing season, past the festive roadside stands filled with apples, pumpkins, & cider. ♥ We stopped at wonderful tiny restaurants in old houses with slanted floors & ate delicious soups, hot puddings bathed in cream & bowls of fresh raspberries. We saw the geese flying in formation & smoke curling out of 200-year-old chimneys. New England holds the key to American history; it can also hold the key to your heart, especially in the fall. ♥

CELEBRATE AUTUMN: Put a pumpkin on your porch ⌐ use bowls of nuts & apples to decorate.
        🎃 Get the last of those vine-ripened sweet summer tomatoes & make your own tomato sauce to freeze for winter. Visit an apple farm ⌐ make applesauce & can it for Christmas presents And don't forget the blueberries & raspberries to freeze for winter pies.
        🎃 Have a morning tea party ⌐ light the fire ⌐ float small apples studded with cloves in hot cider. Serve home-made toast with honey butter & breakfast sausage cooked in maple syrup.

~Fall~

🎃 Plan ahead & think of some really special & fitting words to bless your Thanksgiving dinner & family.

🎃 Make soups — they bubble softly, warm your house with delicious aromas & comfort your tummy on a chilly night.

🎃 Start planning for next summer's family reunion. Make & send invitations so that all, near & far, will have time to plan to come.

🎃 Save all your wine corks. You can glue them onto a piece of plywood to make a wonderful corkboard for your kitchen.

🎃 Go to a football game — take a warm blanket & a thermos of hot chocolate to share. (Hot chocolate is delicious with peppermint schnapps in it.)

🎃 Make a picture wall of family & friends. Mount your photos on matte board with spray glue. People love looking at them.

🎃 Halloween: I have a black iron cat I like to put on the porch with the scary-faced carved pumpkins — or get a big cardboard skeleton for your door. Have a Halloween dinner — serve the "Jack Be Little" Tiny Pumpkins on p.57, & Witches' Brew, p.136.

"An' all us other children,
   when the supper things is done,
We set around the kitchen fire
   an' has the mostest fun
A-list'nin' to the witch-tales
   'at Annie tells about,
An' the gobble-uns 'at gits you
   Ef you Don't Watch Out !"
                   James Whitcomb Riley

GIFT IDEAS
for those who have "Everything"

Antique stores are wonderful places — when you see some small perfect little thing, buy it & tuck it away for just the right moment. ♥ More ideas:

Tickets to something special — a play, concert or ball game.

Trees: cherry, walnut, lemon, apple or pear. There are also some elegant little miniatures to grow inside.

Homemade tapes of their favorite music.

One especially gorgeous sterling silver serving piece wrapped in beautiful paper. (I love the tissue paper Victoria's Secret uses & save it for this.)

An old book — something of interest to the person — beautifully bound & papered.

Their favorite newspaper — issued on the day & year of their birth.

Save all your Sweetheart roses & dry them by hanging upside down. Give potpourri in a delicate glass bowl & include lots of the dried roses.

Enlarged photos of themselves or their loved ones (kids, boat, car?).

A beautiful old flowered teacup & saucer.

For Christmas this year I was given a darling bowl with crocus getting ready to bloom — it's now the middle of January & I check on it & admire it everyday. I just love it — a kind of continuing present. (Thanks, Peg♥)

SOUPS

To love what you do and feel that it matters —
how could anything be more fun? " ♥
Katharine Graham

SPLIT PEA SOUP

Serves Ten

A hearty soup to warm the tummy ♥.

2 large ham hocks
1 lb. split peas, rinsed
2 med. onions, chopped
3 stalks celery, chopped
3 carrots, chopped
1 clove garlic, minced

1 bay leaf
½ tsp. oregano
1 tsp. dry mustard
1 tsp. salt
8 c. cold water
5 strips bacon

Put everything but the bacon in a soup pot. Bring to a boil, reduce heat, cover & simmer for 2 hours, stirring occasionally. Remove ham hocks, take off meat & cut in pieces. Put the meat back in the soup. Fry up the bacon crisp & either put it in the soup or use it to garnish each serving. ♥ The soup can either be thinned with water or thickened by boiling away liquid with the lid off.

"There are fairies at the bottom of our garden!"
♥ Rose Fyleman

78

WATERCRESS & ORANGE SOUP

Serves Four

Serve this refreshing cold soup for the first course in a springtime dinner. The orange flavor is subtle & elegant. ♥

2 bunches watercress, chopped
2½ c. chicken broth
2 Tbsp. fresh chives, chopped
1 egg yolk
1 c. heavy cream
freshly ground pepper
1 c. fresh orange juice
2 Tbsp. Grand Marnier

Simmer watercress, chicken broth & chives together for ½ hour. Blend mixture in food processor till smooth. Reheat mixture (don't boil). Whisk egg yolk & cream together. Mix a little of the hot soup into the cream; pour the cream into the soup & stir until hot. Grind over pepper to taste. Refrigerate soup until well chilled. Just before serving stir in fresh orange juice & Grand Marnier. If you like, sprinkle on fresh chives, or use a thin slice of orange or a sprig of fresh watercress for garnish. ♥

"One day in the country / Is worth a month in town." ♥ Christina Rossetti

CHINOIS SOUP

Serves Five

The little ginger-filled crepes tied up with chives look darling floating in this delicious light broth. This looks complicated to make, but it's really not. The filled crepes can be made ahead. ♥

Crepes

Makes 10 5" crepes

1 beaten egg
½ c. milk

scant ½ c. flour
1 Tbsp. melted butter

Add milk to beaten egg; gradually whisk in flour, till smooth. Beat in butter. Lightly oil 7" sauté pan, HEAT till moderately hot. Pour about 3 Tbsp. batter into pan & quickly swirl to coat bottom. Lightly brown, turn to cook other side. Finish all & make

Filling

3/4 c. waterchestnuts
4 green onions, tops only
3 tsp. fresh ginger
10 long whole chives

Mince finely first 3 ingredients. Put 1 tsp. of mixture in center of each crepe. Tie into little bag with whole chive.

Soup

5 c. homemade or canned chicken broth
1½ Tbsp. light soy sauce
2 tsp. sesame oil
Bring all ingredients to a boil. Put 2 filled crepes into each soup bowl — ladle hot soup over & serve.

VEGETABLE & CHEESE SOUP

Serves Four

Everybody loves this soup. ♡ It's creamy with little bits of vegetables. I like to serve it with either cucumber sandwiches or buttered French bread & radishes. ♡

2 Tbsp. butter
1 leek, chopped
2 carrots, sliced
1 sm. onion, chopped
1 stalk celery, chopped
1 Tbsp. cornstarch
3 Tbsp. flour
2 c. milk

1 13¾-oz. can chicken broth
1 ⅓ c. grated cheddar cheese
½ tsp. salt
2 Tbsp. parsley, minced
2 Tbsp. chives, chopped
pinch of cayenne pepper
⅛ tsp. baking soda

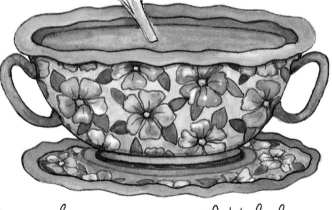

Melt butter in large saucepan. Add leek, carrots, onion & celery; sauté slowly until soft. Stir in cornstarch & flour, blending well. In another pan heat milk & broth together; add to vegetables. Cook over medium heat until thickened. Purée mixture in food processor. Return mixture to saucepan; add cheese, salt, parsley, chives & cayenne. Stir till cheese is melted. Add baking soda to lighten. Serve hot. ♡

PUMPKIN SOUP

Serves Eight

A delicious autumn soup that looks wonderful when served in a big hollowed~out pumpkin. ♥

2 pumpkins, 1 lg. & 1 med.
2 med. onions, chopped
2 Tbsp. butter
1 Tbsp. flour
3 c. chicken broth

½ tsp. nutmeg
½ tsp. ginger
1 c. heavy cream
freshly ground
  pepper

Set aside lg. pumpkin till later. Cut the med. one in half; discard seeds & strings. Cut it in large pieces & steam till tender. Cool & scrape pumpkin away from shell. You'll need 3 c. mashed pumpkin, set aside. In a heavy large saucepan, sauté the onions very slowly in the butter till tender. Sprinkle in flour, stir & cook 2~3 min. Gradually whisk in chicken broth; add the 3 c. pumpkin & cook gently for 15 min. Add spices & cool slightly. In batches, purée the soup in blender or food processor till smooth. Put it back into saucepan, add cream & heat through but don't boil. Refrigerate till ready to serve. When ready, cut off top of lg. pumpkin, scrape out the insides. Pour the reheated soup into the pumpkin, sprinkle with pepper & a little more nutmeg & serve. ♥

WILD RICE & NUT SOUP

Serves Four to Six

Subtly colorful with an elegant broth and a crunch of wild rice & almonds. ♥ Good!

FOR AMY GUIP
RICK PATRICK
9/91   AMY MELLEN
        GREG

½ c. wild rice
2 Tbsp. shallots, minced
2 Tbsp. butter
½ c. mushrooms, sliced
¼ c. unbleached flour
4 c. chicken broth
¼ c. carrots, grated
¼ c. slivered almonds, toasted
1 c. half & half
2 Tbsp. dry sherry
chopped parsley for garnish

Add wild rice to 2 c. boiling water, cover, & simmer 45 min. Toast the almonds in a little butter; drain on paper towels. In a large saucepan sauté shallots slowly in butter till soft. Add mushrooms, sauté 2 min. Stir in flour; gradually add chicken broth, stirring till slightly thickened. Add rice, almonds, & carrots. Simmer 5 min. Add half & half & sherry; heat through (don't boil). Sprinkle over parsley ♥.

♥   ♥   ♥   ♥

"I can live for two months on a good compliment." ♥ Mark Twain

83   * Really good fall soup
        Greg
9/91 dinner Amy/Rick Patrick/Amy Mellen

CHILLED CUCUMBER & TOMATO SOUP

Serves Four

I liken this to gazpacho, but creamy. It's wonderful in the summer.

3 cucumbers, peeled & coarsely chopped
¼ c. parsley (no stems)
½ c. green onions, chopped
2 cloves garlic, minced
1 c. tomato juice (or V-8)
1 c. chicken broth
3 Tbsp. cider vinegar
2 c. sour cream
salt & freshly ground pepper, to taste
sliced cherry tomatoes, for garnish

Put the cucumbers, parsley, green onions, garlic, tomato juice, chicken broth, & vinegar into food processor & blend well. Pour into large bowl; add sour cream & salt & pepper to taste & mix together. Serve, garnished with sliced cherry tomatoes. ♥

"A knight errant who turns mad for a reason deserves neither merit nor thanks. The thing is to do it without cause."

Miguel de Cervantes

GARLIC SOUP
Serves Four

Garlic's good for you! ♥

20 cloves garlic (yug! 20)
2 onions, sliced
1½ Tbsp. olive oil
3 c. tomatoes, peeled & chopped
2 c. tomato juice
2 c. beef broth
8 ½" slices French-bread baguette, toasted
4 oz. Swiss cheese, grated

Blanch garlic cloves in boiling water 30 seconds, rinse in cold water, drain, peel, slice thin. In a large saucepan, sauté the onions in oil till soft & golden, about 15 min. Add garlic, tomatoes, & tomato juice. Bring to boil; reduce heat, cover and simmer 30 min. Add the beef broth — bring to boil, ladle into ovenproof bowls. Top with toast, then cheese. Put into 450° oven till cheese is melted. Serve ♥

"My kitchen is a mystical place, a kind of temple for me. It is a place where the surfaces seem to have significance, where the sounds and odors carry meaning that transfers from the past and bridges to the future."
Pearl Bailey ♥

BORSCHT

Serves Six

Very easy, beautiful color & good for you. Serve it with pickled herring in sour cream, red onion slices & some good pumpernickel bread. A little Russian feast. ♥

2 c. beets, peeled & chopped
1 lg. onion, chopped
2 carrots, thinly sliced
2 celery ribs, thinly sliced
2 c. cabbage, shredded
2 lg. potatoes, diced
4 c. beef broth
4 c. water
2 c. tomato purée
2 cloves garlic, minced
1 bay leaf
salt & freshly ground pepper
sour cream for garnish, opt.

Combine all ingredients, except salt, pepper, & sour cream, in large soup pot. Bring to a boil & simmer about 1½ hours. Remove bay leaf, add salt & pepper to taste & serve with a spoonful of sour cream. ♥

" Soup is sensitive. You don't catch steak hanging around when you're poor and sick, do you?" ♥ Judith Martin

Turkey Soup

Waste not, want not. ♥ We had a 22 lb. bird this year, which gave me about 20 cups of stock — so I froze 10 for later & last night I made the first batch. ♥

The Stock: Pick all the meat off the carcass & reserve. Put the carcass in a big pot & add a couple of carrots, 1 onion, 2 stalks celery, a handful of parsley — all unpeeled, but washed & coarsely chopped. Add a few peppercorns, a bay leaf or two. Add water to cover, boil; then cover and simmer 6—10 hours. Strain, refrigerate overnight, uncovered. Remove fat from top of stock.

Soup

10 c. stock
1 med. onion, chopped
2 stalks celery, chopped
2 carrots, chopped
1 tbsp. olive oil
1 tbsp. butter
turkey meat, chopped

¼ c. parsley, chopped
1 tsp. basil
½ tsp. thyme
½ tsp. sage
4 oz. egg noodles
salt & pepper

Bring stock to boil, taste for strength — if weak, boil down. Sauté onion, celery & carrots in oil & butter. Add rest of ingredients to stock. When noodles are done, add vegetables & serve. ♥ This is great "diet food" after holiday debaucheries ♥.

"So once in every year we throng
 Upon a day apart,
So praise the Lord with feast and song
 In thankfulness of heart." ♥
Arthur Guiterman

87

HOT APPLE SOUP

Serves Four

You can even serve this soup for brunch — it's a Fall soup, when apples are a part of the celebration ♥.

4 green apples (Granny Smith)   ½ tsp. cinnamon
4 McIntosh apples   1 c. light cream
2½ c. water   unsweetened whipped
2 Tbsp. lemon juice   cream, for garnish
¼ tsp. nutmeg

Peel, core & quarter apples. Combine all ingredients except cream in saucepan & bring to boil. Simmer 15 min. till apples are soft. Purée; return to pan; add cream & heat through but don't boil. Garnish each serving with a dollop of unsweetened whipped cream & a sprinkle of cinnamon. ♥

"On a windy day let's go flying
There may be no trees to rest on
There may be no clouds to ride
But we'll have our wings and the
wind will be with us
That's enough for me, that's enough
for me."   Yoko Ono

MANY MUSHROOMS SOUP

Serves Four to Six

There are so many kinds of mushrooms available today, shapes, colors & textures. Take your pick for this beautiful soup. 🤍

CHRISTMAS '91

3 Tbsp. butter   3 c. chicken broth
3 Tbsp. oil   ¼ c. white port /SHERRY
1 clove garlic, minced   2 Tbsp. tomato paste
1 onion, chopped   ½ c. parsley, minced
1 lb. mixed mushrooms   pepper, to taste
   (oyster, morels, porcini,
    enoki, brown or common — your choice)

Melt butter & oil in lg. saucepan. Sauté garlic & onion slowly over low heat, 10 min. Add sliced mushrooms, cover & cook over med. heat 5 min. Add broth, port & tomato paste. Simmer 10 min. Add parsley & freshly ground pepper. Serve. 🤍

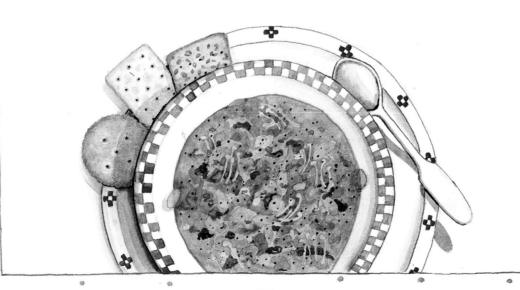

89

AVOCADO SOUP

Serves Four

This is a delicious chilled summer soup — and really easy to make — no hot stove to deal with.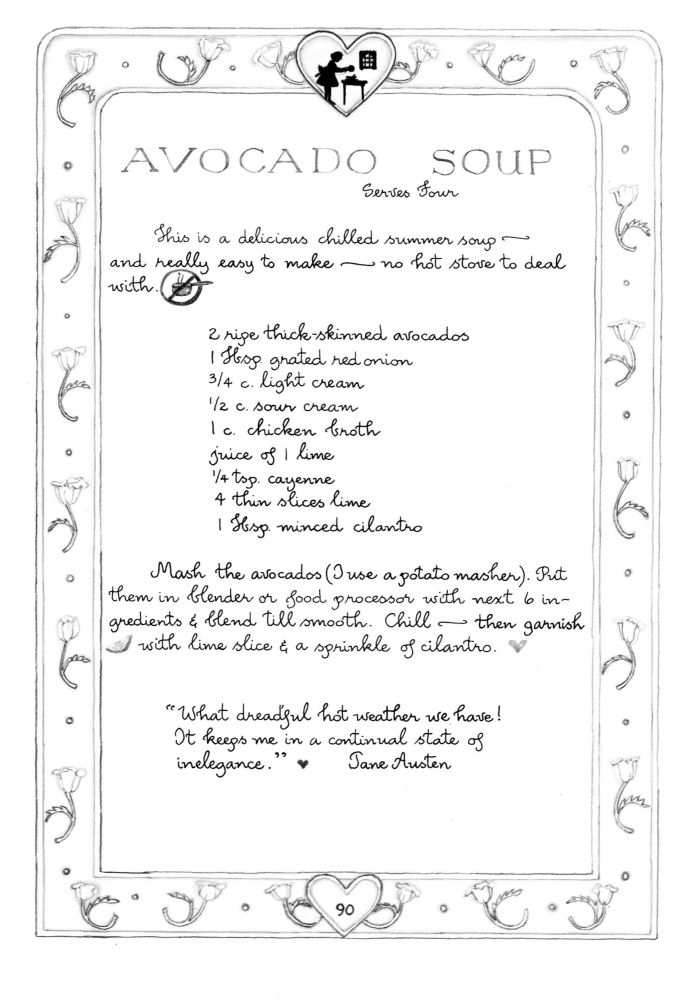

2 ripe thick-skinned avocados
1 Tbsp. grated red onion
3/4 c. light cream
1/2 c. sour cream
1 c. chicken broth
juice of 1 lime
1/4 tsp. cayenne
4 thin slices lime
1 Tbsp. minced cilantro

Mash the avocados (I use a potato masher). Put them in blender or food processor with next 6 ingredients & blend till smooth. Chill — then garnish with lime slice & a sprinkle of cilantro. ♥

"What dreadful hot weather we have!
It keeps me in a continual state of
inelegance." ♥   Jane Austen

LOBSTER BISQUE

Serves Six

A delicate peach-colored soup, not as heavy as some I've tasted but still extravagant & wonderful 🖤.

3 Tbsp. butter
1/2 c. shallots, minced
4 c. chicken broth
1 bay leaf
1/4 tsp. thyme
3 Tbsp. flour

2 Tbsp. tomato paste
3/4 c. dry white wine
1 lb. cooked lobster
    meat
1 1/2 c. half & half
1 Tbsp. cognac

Melt butter in lg. saucepan & sauté shallots till tender, over low heat. Meanwhile, bring chicken broth, bay leaf, & thyme to a boil in another pan. Whisk flour into shallot mixture, cook, stirring, 1-2 min. Stir in tomato paste; slowly whisk in boiling broth. Gradually add wine; simmer 10 min., stirring occasionally. Chop lobster meat, reserving a few nice pieces for garnish. Put the chopped meat & soup into food processor & blend. Return to pot, stir in half & half, then cognac. Heat through, garnish with lobster & serve. 🖤

"The advantage of doing one's praising for oneself is that one can lay it on so thick and exactly in the right places."
🖤 Samuel Butler

91

WINTER

Winter in New England is a special treat for me ~ it's when the island is quietest ~ time seems to stand still except for when the holidays roll around & then it goes too quickly. I especially like it because it feels like a time to reflect & work ~ to sit by a warm fire, watch a quiet snowfall with birds & squirrels busy at the feeders. Here are some ideas to help you celebrate winter:

Save all of your children's mittens ~ even if you don't have both of them ~ from when they are babies. By the time they are 6 or 7 you'll have a lovely collection of winter memories to frame & hang on your wall.

Once a month stand in the exact same position outside your home & take a picture of your house & yard. Frame all the pictures together for a wonderful seasonal collage. ★

If you live in snow country, make your Christmas cards by using fresh cranberries & holly to write your message in the snow; photograph it & make as many copies as you'll need. Send them out as postcards. ♥

A tradition I've always loved: Have family and friends join hands at midnight on New Year's Eve & say a special prayer for the coming year. "Auld Lang Syne" by Guy Lombardo is a special touch to help welcome the new year.

For Dad on Valentine's: a personalized card. Put lipstick on you & your little ones ~ everybody kisses the card.

More Winter

Keep a fire burning ~ it's such a nice welcome for holiday guests or anytime. ♥

Put out baskets & bowls of fresh cranberries, bright red apples, lemons studded with cloves, nuts in their shells, potpourri, pomegranates, or fresh holly.

Use brightly colored quilts for tablecloths ~ have lots of candles burning.

For Christmas Eve Dinner hang a stocking on the back of each guest's chair ~ fill with funny & special gifts pertaining to the interests of the guest. Open them, with coffee & dessert, one at a time.

Simmer herbs & spices for good holiday smells ~ and play "The Nutcracker" at Christmas Brunch.

For the Christmas table tie together tiny bunches of mistletoe with narrow satin ribbons & tuck in a placecard for each guest.

Make sure all your friends get home safely from holiday parties. ♥

The best gifts are handmade ~ gifts of food, knitted, embroidered or quilted things; wooden things & painted & drawn things ~ whatever you're good at. Encourage your children to be creative too.

Sleigh rides, Christmas caroling, tree cutting parties with popcorn & cranberry stringing to follow, old toys for decoration ~ I could go on forever ♥ Merry Xmas!

Memories . . . the food of our childhood; food that meant love ♥

On Valentine's Day we felt especially loved when we woke to a breakfast of hot cereal, tinted pink with food coloring & sprinkled with those little red Cinnamon Hearts. ♥

Jell-O Oranges: Use a 6 oz. pkg. of Jell-O — what kind? RED !! Make according to pkg. instructions except use only 1½ c. boiling water (instead of 2). Hollow out halved oranges & fill with Jell-O. This makes 10 halves. Chill well & serve with a dot of whipped cream.

Purple Cow: a good summer drink — so nice & purple! Put a scoop of vanilla ice cream in a tall glass; fill up halfway with grape juice & top with fizzy water.

Rice Krispie Treats: kids know this is kids' food — but I still like 'em too. Melt ¼ c. butter in large saucepan — add 40 lg. marshmallows & stir till melted. Stir in 5 c. RiceKrispies. Press into 9" x 13" pan & chill.

Adventure Food: when your kids go off on an adventure, a hike, ice skating, or to a football game — make them this hot lunch to take along. Fill a large thermos with hot chili & chopped onions — then tie thread or dental floss around cooked hot dogs & push them down into the chili — leave the strings out. Send along a little bag of buns & napkins. ♥

Christmas: make cookies together to leave for Santa. Tie "hay" (grass, weeds, whatever) into a bundle for Rudolph.

Some-Mores: toast a marshmallow (over a fire). Put thin squares of chocolate on a graham cracker; add marshmallow & another cracker.

Sue's Bag 'O Buns

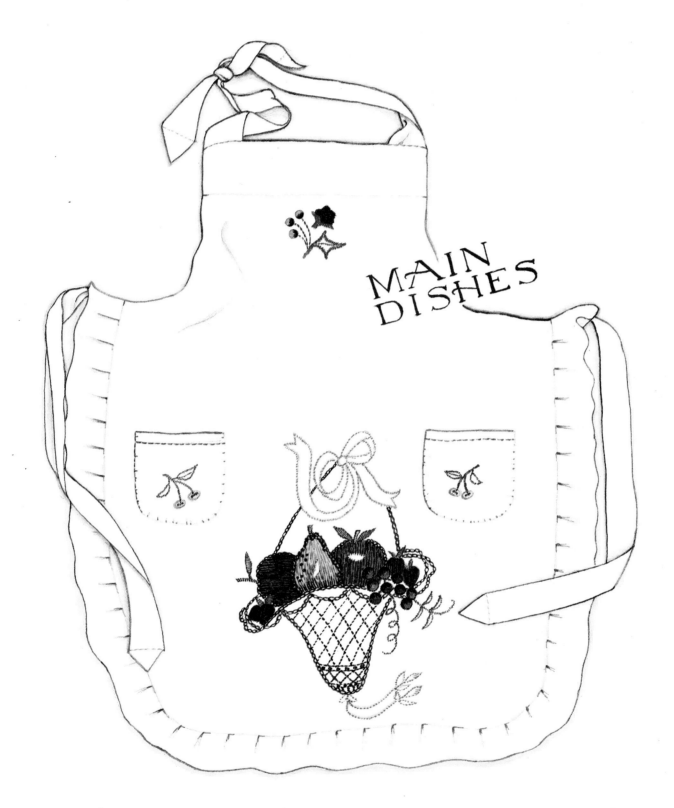

MAIN
DISHES

"I don't want to make money. I just want to be wonderful."
♥ Marilyn Monroe

Chipped Beef on Toast

Serves Six

My Joe likes his toast cut up — mine has to be torn. Such is the "Mom food" mystique — all tied up with childhood memories. ♥

10 oz. dried beef
6 Tbsp. sweet butter
1 c. onion, minced

6 Tbsp. flour
4 c. hot milk
freshly ground pepper

12 slices hearty white bread, toasted

Pour boiling water over beef — let sit 10 min. Rinse, drain & pat dry. (Removes excess salt.) Melt butter in lg saucepan, add onions & cook slowly till tender. Sprinkle in flour & whisk for 1 minute. Slowly whisk in hot milk, stirring till it thickens. Add beef & pepper to taste; heat through. Serve over toast. ♥

Macaroni & Cheese

375° Six Servings

10 oz. elbow macaroni
2 eggs
1 Tbsp. dry mustard

½ tsp. salt
¼ tsp. pepper
2 c. half & half

1 lb. sharp cheddar cheese, grated

Preheat oven to 375° Cook & drain the macaroni. In a large bowl, lightly beat eggs with mustard, salt & pepper. Stir in half & half, then the cheese & then cooked macaroni. Pour into a buttered 2 qt. casserole & bake 25 min. Put it under the broiler 1 minute to make the top brown & a little crisp. ♥

Scalloped Potatoes with Sausages

350° Serves Four

½ lb. breakfast link sausages
4 c. peeled baking potatoes, sliced
½ lg. onion, thinly sliced
salt & pepper

4 Tbsp. butter
4 Tbsp. flour
3 c. hot milk

Brown sausages well; drain on paper towels. Heat oven to 350°. Slice the potatoes very thinly & separate the onion slices into rings. In a buttered 8"x10" baking pan, layer potatoes with onion rings, sprinkling each layer with salt & pepper. In a lg. saucepan, melt butter; whisk in flour; cook briefly. Slowly whisk in hot milk. Pour over potatoes. Cover tightly with foil; bake 1 hour. Remove foil~arrange sausages on top & bake, uncovered, 15 minutes more or until potatoes are tender. ♥

Stuffed Bell Peppers

Preheat oven to 350° Serves Six

6 lg. green peppers
1 lg. onion, chopped
2 ribs celery, diced
3 cloves garlic, minced
2 Tbsp. olive oil
1½ lbs. lean ground beef
⅓ c. tomato paste

1 35-oz. can whole tomatoes,
    drained & chopped
¼ c. parsley, minced
2 tsp. oregano
3 tsp. basil
¼ tsp. red pepper flakes
1 tsp. Worcestershire sauce

½ lb. sharp cheddar, in ½" cubes

Halve peppers lengthwise; remove seeds & membranes. Blanch in boiling water 2 min.; drain. In lg. skillet, sauté onion, celery, & garlic 5 min. Add beef & brown; stir in remaining in-gredients. Fill peppers, place on oiled cookie sheet; bake 30 min. Serve. ♥

LEMON NOODLES

400°   Serves Eight

Perfect with fish, but that's not all ~ this stuff is delicious ~ one of my mainstays! Make it all ~ if there's any left over you're going to want it ♥.

1 lb. spaghetti
¼ lb. butter
1 pt. sour cream
juice of one juicy lemon

1 tsp. grated lemon peel
freshly ground pepper
¼ c. minced parsley
Parmesan cheese, to taste

Preheat oven to 400°. Cook the noodles in boiling water; drain & put in baking dish. Melt butter in a small saucepan; remove from heat. Stir in sour cream, lemon juice & lemon peel. Pour over pasta, toss & bake 20~25 minutes. Remove from oven, sprinkle on lots of freshly ground pepper, minced parsley & Parmesan cheese. Toss & eat ♥.

"Great art is as irrational as great music.
It is mad with its own loveliness."
♥ George Jean Nathan

ANGEL HAIR and SHRIMP

Serves Two

This is one of those recipes you never really have to measure — just do it to your own taste & make it for as many as you need to feed. ❤→

6 extra-large shrimp
angel hair pasta, ¼ lb.
1 clove garlic, minced
2 Tbsp. olive oil

1 Tbsp. fresh basil, minced
1 c. tomato, chopped
salt & freshly ground
    pepper, to taste

Peel & devein the shrimp. Cook the pasta in boiling water just till done; drain, rinse in cold water & set aside. Put 1 Tbsp. oil in skillet, add garlic & cook until light brown. Add basil, tomato & salt & pepper to taste. Cook over medium heat, stirring occasionally. Meanwhile add 1 Tbsp. oil to another skillet & sauté shrimp 5~7 minutes, careful not to overcook. Add the pasta to the tomato mixture & heat through. Put the pasta on serving plates, top with shrimp & serve. ❤↗

"Three may keep a secret, if two of them are dead."
            Benjamin Franklin ❤

LINGUINI AND GRILLED SAUSAGES

Serves Four

I have to thank my high school friend Michael I. Ferejohn, professor of philosophy; cook extraordinaire, for this easy & different pasta dish ♥.

2~3 sausages per person
1 c. black olives, pitted
½ c. chopped parsley
4 anchovy fillets
¼ c. white wine
½ lb. lg. white mushrooms

olive oil
2/3 lb. linguini
3 Tbsp. butter
juice of 1 lemon
Parmesan cheese

Use your favorite kind of sausage, or better yet, try 2 or 3 different kinds. Put them on the grill or brown them in a skillet. Put water on to boil for pasta. Put olives, parsley & anchovies into blender or food processor & chop finely. Add wine & set aside. Thinly slice the mushrooms. Heat a small amount of oil in large skillet to very hot. Add mushrooms & cook quickly over hot flame to seal juices. Start cooking the pasta; drain when done. When mushrooms are crisp, lower heat, add the butter, then the olive/wine mixture—heat through, but don't cook. Remove from heat, add lemon juice & toss with cooked pasta. Add Parmesan cheese to taste & serve with sausages. ♥ Try this with heated French-bread rolls & some good mustard. ♥

SPARERIBS & JUICE ♥

275° Serves Four

My mom called us "wild Indians" sometimes, & never did
we look the part more than when we were devouring her
wonderful spareribs & juice. She has a picture of us all
around the table during one of these feasts ~ my poor
dad has a look on his face that clearly says "Must you
take a picture NOW?" But the rest of us are smiling,
with enough "juice" on our faces, hands & clothes to make
a whole other dinner. This was an often-requested
birthday dinner & was served with garden corn on
the cob dripping with butter & fluffy mashed potatoes
WITH lumps. For dessert ~ watermelon ~ served curbside ♥.

Pork ribs for four
2 c. pineapple juice
½ c. catsup
2 Tbsp. steak sauce
2 Tbsp. brown sugar
1 Tbsp. white vinegar
1 tsp. ground mustard
3 cloves minced garlic (opt.)

Put the ribs in a roasting pan & into a 275° oven for 2
hours. Pour off fat. Mix together all remaining ingredients & pour over the ribs. Bake 1 hour more. Serve in
a large bowl surrounded with juice. ♥

SOFT~SHELL CRABS

I cannot fathom WHY, in some restaurants, this delicacy is served mushy — it's so easy to make them crisp & delicious. ♥ You can buy them frozen (already cleaned) & eat them whole.

soft~shell crabs ~ 2 to 3 per person
sprigs of fresh thyme (opt.)
flour for dredging
cooking oil ~ ¼"
chopped parsley
lemon wedges

Shaw, rinse & dry the crabs. Tuck a tiny sprig of thyme under the shell of each crab (if you like). Dredge them in flour. Heat the oil in a large skillet — you'll want it very hot — put the crabs in the pan (don't crowd them) & fry hot & fast, about 5 minutes, till brown & crisp. Serve with a sprinkle of parsley & the lemon wedges. ♥

"Who's your fat friend?" (Of George, Prince of Wales.) ♥ "Beau" Brummell

STEAMED CLAMS

Makes 4 dozen

This can be a lovely light summer dinner served with a salad & some French bread. ♥

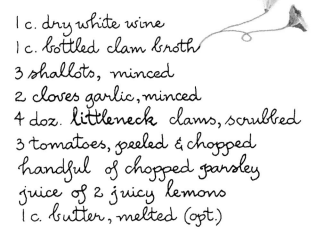

1 c. dry white wine
1 c. bottled clam broth
3 shallots, minced
2 cloves garlic, minced
4 doz. littleneck clams, scrubbed
3 tomatoes, peeled & chopped
handful of chopped parsley
juice of 2 juicy lemons
1 c. butter, melted (opt.)

Combine the wine, broth, shallots & garlic in a large soup pot; bring to boil; add clams. Cover & steam just till they open. Dip the tomatoes in boiling water for 15 seconds — skin will slip off. Chop them finely. Put clams in serving bowl; sprinkle over tomatoes, parsley, & lemon juice. Serve with melted butter for dipping if you like ♥.

"And you shall wander hand in
hand with love in summer's
wonderland;
Go down to Kew in lilac-time
(it isn't far from London!)"
♥ Alfred Noyes

SESAME NOODLES
CHIEN NOIR

Serves Six

The Black Dog Tavern on Martha's Vineyard serves many wonderful dishes, but this has to be my all-time favorite ♥ Thank you, Charlie Esposito!

¼ c. tahini
¼ c. warm water
¼ c. soy sauce (or tamari)
¼ c. vegetable oil
2 Tbsp. sugar

2 Tbsp. cider vinegar
2 cloves garlic, minced
1½ Tbsp. chili oil
2 tsp. sesame oil
½ c. green onions
16 oz. thin udon noodles

Look for any unfamiliar ingredients at your health food store. Whisk together tahini & warm water; whisk in soy sauce, vegetable oil, sugar, vinegar, garlic, chili oil & sesame oil. Finely chop green onions. Cook the noodles according to package; lightly coat them with sauce, tossing gently. Sprinkle on green onions & serve. ♥ Best hot or at room temperature. Try Chinese egg noodles if you can't find the udon. ♥

" My little old dog: A heart-beat at my feet."
♥ Edith Wharton

CHICKEN IN CHERRY SAUCE

Serves Six

♥ A special company dinner—an old recipe from home.

1 med. onion, minced
2 Tbsp. butter
2 Tbsp. oil
4 whole, boned & skinned chicken breasts, halved

more butter
1 can pitted dark cherries
3 Tbsp. cornstarch
2 c. chicken stock
¼ c. sherry

flour for dredging, mixed with salt & pepper

♥ Preheat oven to 200°. Slowly sauté onion in butter & oil, about 15 min. Remove onion from pan with slotted spoon & reserve. Pound chicken breasts to achieve uniform thickness, dredge in flour. Add more butter to skillet, making 4 Tbsp. Cook breasts, in batches, 2-3 min. each side, till just cooked through. Remove to platter & keep in warm oven. Drain cherries; reserve juice. Combine juice, cornstarch & stock —pour into the hot skillet & scrape up bits in pan. Boil 3 min.; add reserved onions, cherries & sherry. Heat through. Pour some sauce over the chicken breasts & pass the rest in a sauceboat. ♥

"Father, I cannot tell a lie. I did it with my little hatchet."
♥ George Washington

105

Sun-Dried
TOMATO PESTO

Makes 1 cup; serves four

Quick & easy — all the good things: garlic, sun-dried tomatoes, Parmesan cheese, herbs . . . all together to make this delicious spicy pasta sauce. ♥

1/4 c. almonds, chopped
4~6 oz. sun-dried tomatoes, with oil
1/2 c. olive oil
1/4 c. grated Parmesan cheese
1 Tbsp. garlic, minced
1 Tbsp. onion, minced

1/2 tsp. oregano
1/2 tsp. basil
1/4 tsp. thyme
dash of red pepper
flakes
2 Tbsp. lemon juice

Everything goes into the food processor — whirl till you have a thick, grainy sauce. Cover and refrigerate, or serve immediately: 1/4 c. on each serving of pasta. Pass some additional Parmesan & enjoy. ♥

"I know I have the body of a weak and
feeble woman, but I have the heart and
stomach of a king, and of a king of
England too. . . ."
♥ Queen Elizabeth I

CHICKEN IN PHYLLO

400° Serves Four

Cut into these & out comes the melted cheese. ♥

2 whole, boned, skinned chicken breasts
1 stick butter, melted
1 pkg. phyllo
4 Tbsp. shallots, minced
1 tsp. sage
4 oz. jack cheese

Preheat oven to 400°. Halve chicken breasts & pound flat. Melt butter. Layer 4 sheets phyllo, buttering each sheet. On each chicken breast sprinkle 1 Tbsp. shallots & ¼ tsp. sage. Lay 1 oz. cheese on each breast & roll up. Place breast in the middle of the phyllo, at one end; roll once, fold in sides, brush with butter & continue rolling, buttering as you go. Lay all on ungreased cookie sheet & bake 25 min., till browned. Serve. ♥

The Leader of the Pack

"If a recipe cannot be written on the face of a 3×5 card, off with its head."
♥ Helen Nearing

(Not Just the Regular) STEW

Serves Eight

Made with good-quality beef, fresh vegetables, red wine, & herbs; served with hot crusty French bread, a dry red wine & a crisp salad—it's perfect for a frosty night at home. ♥

2 lbs. tenderloin, cut in 1-inch cubes

flour for dredging

2 tbsp. each butter & oil

2 cloves garlic, minced

salt & freshly ground pepper

2 c. dry red wine

2 beef bouillon cubes dissolved in 2 c. boiling water

1 baking potato, grated

1 onion, peeled & studded with 2 cloves

2 tsp. thyme

1 bay leaf

8 red potatoes, unpeeled & quartered

8 carrots, sliced

4 stalks celery, sliced

8 tiny white onions

1 or 2 c. tomato juice

handful of fresh parsley, finely chopped

Dredge meat in flour. Melt butter & oil in large pot; add garlic. Cook the beef just to rare; remove from pot & refrigerate. Add wine & bouillon to pan & scrape up bits stuck to bottom. Add potato, onion, thyme & bay leaf. Bring to boil, cover & simmer 1 hour. Add potatoes, carrots, celery & onions; simmer ½ hr. Add tomato juice, as necessary for nice gravy. Add beef cubes, reheat; toss in parsley & serve. ♥

CHICKEN & DUMPLINGS

Serves Six

My grandmother is one of 10 children & grew up in that peaceful time before T.V. & radio ♥. On Sundays, after church, they would gather in the 3rd floor music room of their Iowa home to sing & be musical ♪. Afterwards they'd sit down to a big chicken dinner "with all the fixin's." Chicken & Dumplings was a favorite. ♥

8 pieces chicken (about 5 lb.)
3 ribs celery, sliced
4 carrots, sliced
1 lg. onion, chopped
Freshly ground pepper
2 tsp. salt
2 Tbsp. parsley, minced
2 tsp. thyme

½ tsp. rosemary

2 c. unbleached flour
1 tsp. salt
3 tsp. baking powder
2 Tbsp. parsley, minced
¼ c. shortening (Crisco)
¾ c. whole milk

Wash & dry the chicken. In a large pot, brown the pieces in a little oil. Put in the vegetables & herbs; add water to cover & bring to a boil. Reduce heat & simmer 20 min. Meanwhile, make the dumplings. Combine flour, salt, baking powder & parsley. With pastry cutter, cut in the shortening till it resembles coarse meal. Stir in milk with a fork just to make dough hold together. Drop the dough onto simmering broth, by tablespoonfuls. Cover & continue simmering 20 min. more without peeking. To serve, put chicken piece in a wide soup bowl with dumplings & ladle over hot broth. ♥

"It is a great art to saunter."
♥ Henry David Thoreau

VEAL WITH DUMPLINGS

375° Serves Eight

Yes, there's canned soup in this — but I don't care — it's GOOD. It's also the dish I requested for my birthday dinners ! (Ultimate Mom Food ♥.)

Veal

2 lb. veal cutlets, cut in 1" pieces
flour
4 Tbsp. butter
salt & pepper
1 c. water

1 lg. onion, sliced
2 Tbsp. butter
1 can cream of chicken soup
1 3/4 c. water

Roll veal in flour & brown quickly in butter. Add salt, pepper, & water; simmer 30 min. Meanwhile, in another pan, slowly cook onion in butter. Pour the veal into a 9"x13" casserole; arrange onion on top. In the veal skillet, bring the soup & water to a boil & pour over veal. Make the

Dumplings

2 c. flour
4 tsp. baking powder
1/2 tsp. salt
1 tsp. poultry seasoning

1 Tbsp. poppy seeds
1/4 c. salad oil
1 c. milk
3 Tbsp. melted butter
3/4 c. bread crumbs

Preheat oven to 375°. Mix together first 5 ingredients. Stir in oil & milk. Mix melted butter & bread crumbs — roll rounded tablespoons of batter into bread crumb mixture and place on top of veal. Bake 20 min.

Sauce (which, believe it or not, is delicious!)

1 c. sour cream
1 c. cream of chicken soup

Combine & heat. Pass separately to be poured over dumplings & veal ♥.

STEAK AU POIVRE

Serves Two

Devil food ~ so good & so bad! But outrageously delicious ♥.

1-1½ Tbsp. cracked black peppercorns
2 tenderloin steaks, at least 1¼" thick
2 Tbsp. butter
1 Tbsp. shallots, minced

2 Tbsp. cognac
2 Tbsp. red wine
¼ c. beef broth
2 Tbsp. heavy cream

Crack the peppercorns in mortar & pestle or with rolling pin on board. Press them into steaks. Heat butter in heavy skillet. Sear steaks over med. high heat, both sides, turning with tongs. Reduce heat to med. & cook, turning often, till desired doneness. Remove meat from pan & keep warm. Add shallots to pan & sauté a minute or so. Add cognac & wine ~ boil 2 min., stirring. Add beef broth & boil 2 more min., scraping up bits from pan. Stir in cream, heat through but don't boil. Pour sauce over steaks & serve. ♥

VICTIM LEAVING
TOWN

MIXED SHELLFISH

400°

This elegant dish takes only minutes to prepare. ♥

For each serving:

> 2 jumbo shrimp, peeled & cleaned
> 6 tiny scallops, or 2 large,
>   cut in bite-sized pieces
> 4 pieces cooked lobster meat
> 1 Tbsp. shallots, minced
> 1 Tbsp. parsley, minced
> olive oil
> dry vermouth
> lemon wedge

Preheat oven to 400°. Put the fish into a shell dish. Sprinkle on shallots & parsley; dribble over a little olive oil & a splash of vermouth. Bake about 10 min. Serve with lemon wedge. ♥ Be very careful not to overcook. ♥

♥   ♥   ♥   ♥   ♥

A recipe for fish baked in ashes: "No cheese, no nonsense! Just place it tenderly in fig leaves and tie them on top with a string; then push it under hot ashes, bethinking thee wisely of the time when it is done, and burn it not up." ♥ Archestratus, 4th century B. C.

SOLE MEUNIÈRE
Serves Four

Your basic fabulous fish dish ♥

2 lb. sole fillets, very fresh
unbleached flour
2 Tbsp. vegetable oil
6 Tbsp. butter
¼ c. minced parsley
juice of 1 juicy lemon

Rinse the sole & pat dry. Dredge in flour to coat; shake off excess. Heat oil plus 2 Tbsp. butter in skillet till hot. Brown fillets quickly, turning once. Remove to warm platter. Add remaining butter to skillet; when it begins to bubble, scrape up brown bits in pan & remove from heat. Stir in parsley & lemon juice. Pour over fillets & serve at once. ♥

"Everything that lives in water is seductive." ♥   Jean~Paul Aron

DUCK À L'ORANGE

375° Serves Two, maybe Three

Easy to do — if it's for a special evening, get some paper
frills for the legs — duck ankles are notoriously thin ♥.

a 5~6 lb. duck
2 oranges
1 lemon
3 Tbsp. red wine vinegar
1 Tbsp. sugar
2 Tbsp. brandy
¼ c. hot chicken stock
thin orange & lemon slices, for garnish

Roast the duck in preheated 375° oven, on a rack, for
20~25 min. per pound. Prick the skin several times
to release fat & baste every 15 min. Meanwhile, grate
the rind of the oranges & lemon; blanch in boiling
water 20 seconds; drain; set aside. In a small
saucepan, simmer vinegar & sugar till sugar melts,
turns a little brown & thickens slightly. Add the
juice of the oranges & the lemon; simmer briefly & add
the blanched rinds. When duck is done, remove to
hot platter & decorate with orange & lemon slices (paper
frills for duck ankles, if desired). Allow duck to sit
15 min. before carving. From duck pan, pour off all
fat, leaving only the brown juices. Over high
heat, add brandy & chicken stock, scraping
brown bits from pan; pour into orange
sauce. Reheat & serve in a sauceboat. ♥

114

PIZZA

This is made with real French bread & you'll have enough dough here for four 10" pies. Eat 1, freeze 3, & you'll always be ready for the craving you're sure to have from now on. ♥

Bread

1 pkg. dry yeast
2 c. lukewarm water
2 tsp. salt

1 Tbsp. sugar
4~5 c. flour
olive oil

Dissolve yeast in water. Let stand 5 min. Stir in salt & sugar. Gradually mix in the flour, till it won't take anymore. Knead on floured board 3~4 min. Let rise 1 hr. in greased bowl, covered, in a warm spot. Punch down, divide into four pieces. Wrap 3 separately & freeze. Stretch remaining piece into 10 inch round. Put on buttered baking sheet & let rise, covered, 45 min. Brush with olive oil. Bake at 400° for 12~15 min. with a pan of boiling water on lower rack. ♥

Filling

1½ broccoli, cut small
1~2 tomatoes, sliced
1 clove garlic, minced
½ tsp. oregano
½ tsp. rosemary
½ tsp. basil

sprinkle of red pepper flakes
5 sun-dried tomatoes, chopped
4 oz. brie, thinly sliced
8 kalamata olives, chopped
Parmesan cheese
freshly ground pepper

Steam broccoli till tender. Put tomatoes on baked pie, then broccoli, & rest of ingredients in order. Broil till cheese melts. Serve ♥. Any group of ingredients that sounds good to you, please try. In the summer try tomatoes with lots of fresh basil & Montrachet cheese. ♥

Little Dinners

My own tastes lean away from the "main dish" & more toward the "little dinner" ⁓ combinations of soups, salads & vegetable dishes. So here are a few of my favorite recipes for little dinners. ♥

Welsh Rabbit
Serves Two

½ lb. sharp cheddar, diced   dash cayenne
1 Tbsp. butter   1 egg, slightly beaten
½ tsp. dry mustard   ½ c. beer
¼ tsp. Worcestershire sauce   4 slices hearty white
                                  bread, toasted

Melt cheese & butter in top of double boiler over boiling water. Stirring constantly, add mustard, Worcestershire, & cayenne. Beat in egg; stir in beer, & stir till hot. Do not boil. Serve over toast. ♥

Vegetable Quesadillas

For each person: melt a pat of butter in a large skillet over med. heat. Lay a flour tortilla in pan; cover with thinly sliced jack cheese; then sprinkle over a combination of tomatoes, olives, red onion & green pepper, all diced. Put another tortilla on top. Cover pan & cook till cheese is almost melted; carefully flip tortillas & cook other side. Cut it like a pie & serve it with Salsa (p.25) & sour cream. ♥

Little Dinners:

" In giving a dinner, the error is usually on the side of abundance". Thomas Cooper

Rice & Vegetables

For each person: Put about 3/4 c. cooked brown rice in an ovenproof dish. Top with: chopped tomato, grated carrot, finely chopped broccoli, minced green onion, minced parsley, toasted pine nuts, freshly ground pepper — and any other vegetables & herbs you like. Spread grated jack or Muenster cheese over the top. Bake at 350° for ½ hour. ♥

Beans & Rice

Serves Two

1 can beans	garnishes, opt.:
2 c. cooked brown rice	sour cream
3 Tbsp. chopped onion	salsa

Get health food store beans — refried, or what you like; heat them up. Put hot rice on plate, cover with beans, sprinkle over onions. If you like, add a dollop of sour cream & a spoonful of salsa. ♥

Pita Bread Sandwich

Into food processor put cooked chicken, lots of different raw vegetables & herbs, a squeeze of lemon juice, a bit of mustard. Whirl to the consistency of rice. Pile into toasted whole wheat pita bread. ♥

Romance:

A beautiful word that even sounds pretty. And that's what romance is all about — it's a celebration of the senses. ♥ Things that taste, smell, feel, sound, & look wonderful are the stuff romance is made of. It's the celebration of being Alive. If you want a special & romantic time, try to appeal to the 5 senses, throw in a little imagination, and voilà!

A few ideas:

When you and your husband ∧ go on vacation, wire ahead for flowers & champagne to be waiting in your room. ♥
(PAL, FRIEND?)

When it's a car trip, pull out a surprise basket of delights — fruit, cheese, bread & wine. ♥

Plant a romantic garden — an English perennial garden — a traditional herb garden. Use the old-fashioned varieties of flowers — old roses, etc. Plant raspberries. ♥

Do something every year that becomes a tradition. Do sensual food — use crystal & silver, light candles, play appropriate music, have lots of flowers. ♥

Write handwritten letters (not typed) — include photos, cartoons, dried flowers, or quotes. ♥

"Mooshey" beds are romantic — feather pillows, soft comforters, fresh flowered sheets; open nearby windows. ♥

118

Romantic ♥ ♥ ♥

A morning kitchen with the smells of coffee, bacon, & bread. ♥

Cuddling your children. ♥

Cooking with someone you love. ♥

From "A Room with a View," Kiri Te Kanawa singing "O Mio Babbino Caro" (Side one, song one). And, all Mozart. ♥

Eating with your fingers & feeding your lover, your friends, your children, with your fingers. ♥

Wallpaper. ♥

Coming home to a crackling fire. ♥

Fall leaves. ♥

Picnics with baskets, quilts, pillows & wonderful foods. ♥

Lace — curtains, pillows, napkins, clothes. ♥

Love of older people: phone calls, letters, involvement. ♥

Paris, France. It's a _feast_ for the senses! So romantic. New York & London too! ♥

Holding hands. ♥

Breakfast in bed. ♥

Components of a romantic evening: icy oysters, chilled vodka, champagne with a bubble bath, fresh flowers, candles & silk — try it! ♥

"Imagination is more important than knowledge."
♥ Albert Einstein

"If you cannot inspire a woman with love of you, fill her above the brim with love of herself—all that runs over will be yours."
♥ Charles Caleb Colton

Desserts

Life is Short ~
Eat Dessert First

TAPIOCA PUDDING

Serves Eight

Light & delicate—there is something comforting & old-fashioned about this dessert. ♥

4 eggs, separated
3¾ c. whole milk
6 Tbsp. quick tapioca
10 Tbsp. sugar
¼ tsp. salt
2 tsp. vanilla
zest of 1 lemon

Slightly beat egg yolks in heavy saucepan; stir in milk, tapioca, 6 Tbsp. sugar, & salt. Let stand 5 min. Bring to full boil over medium heat, stirring constantly; remove from heat. Beat egg whites till frothy, add remaining 4 Tbsp. sugar, & continue beating till stiff. Add whites, vanilla, & grated lemon rind to hot milk mixture & stir to blend. Pour into 8 individual pudding cups & chill. ♥

"Across the gateway of my heart
I wrote 'No Thoroughfare,'
But love came laughing by, and cried:
'I enter everywhere.'"
♥ Herbert Shipman

LEMON ROLL

375° Serves Ten

A luscious, really beautiful cake ~ it's so soft & delicate it reminds me of a newborn baby ~ you'll see what I mean.* It's easy & it's elegant. ♥

3 eggs, separated	1 tsp. baking powder
1 c. sugar	¼ tsp. salt
6 Tbsp. hot water	grated rind of 1 lemon
1 c. flour	Lemon Filling

powdered sugar

Preheat oven to 375°. Beat egg yolks, add sugar & beat till thick & lemon-colored. Stir in water & dry ingredients. Fold in stiffly beaten egg whites. Add grated rind. Grease a cookie sheet that has a rim (jelly roll pan), line it with waxed paper & grease it again. Pour batter into pan, spreading evenly. Bake 12~15 min. Immediately cut off crisp edges & turn out onto large cloth LIGHTLY covered with powdered sugar. Remove waxed paper. Using the cloth, roll up the cake → ▭ & set aside while you make the filling. When ready, unroll cake, spread on filling & roll back up. Cool completely; transfer to serving dish. Cut with serrated knife ♥.

Lemon Filling

1 c. sugar	Put all ingredients in double
2 eggs	boiler ~ beat well & stir till
2 Tbsp. butter, melted	thick ~ 15-20 min. Cool slightly.
juice & grated rind of 2 lemons	♥

Boston Cream Pie

Makes 8 glorious servings

Well, this is my first "two~pager" & I promise you, it's well worth it! I love traditional foods & this is Boston Cream Pie at its most outrageous: creamy & chocolaty, with a light cake ~ 3 heavenly textures in one. ♥

Cream Filling

2 egg yolks
1½ Tbsp. flour
1 Tbsp. cornstarch
¼ c. powdered sugar

1½ c. whole milk
1 Tbsp. butter
½ c. whipping cream
1 tsp. vanilla

Beat the yolks in a double boiler; stir in flour, cornstarch, sugar, milk & butter. Cook over boiling water about 20 min. till thick, stirring constantly. Chill mixture. When cold, whip the cream with the vanilla & fold together. Refrigerate. ♥

Sponge Cake

3 eggs, separated
¼ c. cold water
3/4 c. sugar
½ tsp. vanilla
¼ tsp. lemon zest

3/4 c. cake flour
¼ tsp. baking powder
⅛ tsp. salt
½ tsp. cream of tartar

Preheat oven to 325°. Separate eggs ~ yolks into lg. bowl, whites into smaller. Beat the yolks for 5 min.;

Continued...

gradually add cold water & beat 1 minute. Add sugar gradually & beat 3 more minutes. Stir in vanilla & lemon zest. In another bowl, mix together flour, baking powder & salt with a fork. Add to yolk mixture in thirds, folding in. Beat the whites with the cream of tartar till they form soft peaks. Fold into yolk mixture. Turn into 2 ungreased 8" cake pans. Bake at 325° for 15~20 min. till golden & springs back to touch. Cool upside down. Run a sharp knife around outside & remove cakes from pan. Refrigerate. When ready to frost (when cream & cake are chilled) make the

Chocolate Icing

2 squares unsweetened chocolate (2 oz.)   1 egg yolk
3/4 c. powdered sugar   3 Tbsp. cream
1 Tbsp. water   ½ tsp. vanilla

Melt chocolate in top of double boiler, remove from heat. Beat in sugar & water at once. Add yolk, beat well. Beat in cream, 1 Tbsp. at a time, then vanilla ♥.

♪ Ta-Daa... ♪

Put the cream filling between cake layers. Spread the chocolate over the top, allowing some to dribble over edges. Keep cake refrigerated. ♥

STRAWBERRY SHORTCAKE

400° Serves Eight

The old-fashioned kind, like Mom used to make ♥.

4 c. unbleached flour
½ c. sugar
2 Tbsp. baking powder
¼ tsp. salt
½ c. butter

1 beaten egg
1¼ c. whole milk
3 c. heavy cream
5 c. strawberries

Wash, hull & halve the berries. Put them in a glass bowl & sprinkle 2 or 3 Tbsp. sugar over. Cover & chill. Turn oven to 400°. Combine first 4 ingredients. Chop butter into pieces & cut into flour mixture till crumbly. Beat in egg & milk. Butter 2 baking sheets. Using ½ c. dough per "biscuit," make 8 4" rounds. Bake 15~17 min. till golden. Whip the cream, adding sugar to taste. Put berries on top of shortcake, then a big dollop of whipped cream. ♥ Best served when short~ cake is warm; you can reheat them. ♥ The berries will be juicier if you crush a few before sugaring & let them sit for an hour before using. ♥

Truffles

A wonderful gift for Christmas or Valentine's Day; truffles are quick & easy to make. Make your after~ dinner coffee more special by serving these melt-in~ your-mouth chocolate morsels alongside. ♥

6 oz. semi~sweet chocolate
2 egg yolks
2/3 c. unsalted butter, softened
1 1/3 c. powdered sugar, sifted
2 tsp. vanilla
1/2 c. walnuts, chopped
unsweetened cocoa powder
2 tsp. crème de menthe or Grand Marnier (opt.)

Over very low heat, slowly melt chocolate in a small saucepan, stirring often. Remove from heat & cool. Cream egg yolks & butter together. Add sugar slowly & blend well. Pour the cooled chocolate into sugar mixture; add vanilla & nuts. Stir. (If using a liqueur, omit vanilla & substitute liqueur) Refrigerate until firm enough to handle. Shape into 1" balls; roll in cocoa; chill. Keep refrigerated till ready to serve. Can be frozen. ♥

ORANGE CAKE

Serves 8~10

To die for. ♥ A real special-occasion cake perfect for spring teas, Mother's Day, showers or a pre-wedding party. ♥

Orange Filling

6 Tbsp. sugar
1½ Tbsp. cornstarch
pinch of salt
½ c. water

½ tsp. grated orange peel
½ c. fresh orange juice
1 egg yolk, slightly beaten
1 Tbsp. butter, melted

½ c. crushed pineapple

In top part of double boiler, over boiling water, mix sugar, cornstarch & salt. Gradually add water, orange peel & juice, then egg yolk. Cook, stirring, till smooth & thick. Fold in butter & pineapple. Chill ♥.

The Cake

4 Tbsp. butter
1 c. sugar
2 eggs, separated

1½ c. flour
2 tsp. baking powder
pinch of salt

½ c. fresh orange juice

Preheat oven to 350°. Cream butter & sugar. Add egg yolks & beat till thick & lemon-colored. With a fork, mix together dry ingredients & add them alternately with the o.j. Fold in stiffly beaten egg whites. Pour into two buttered 8" cake pans & bake at 350° for 20 minutes. Cool completely & remove from pans. ♥

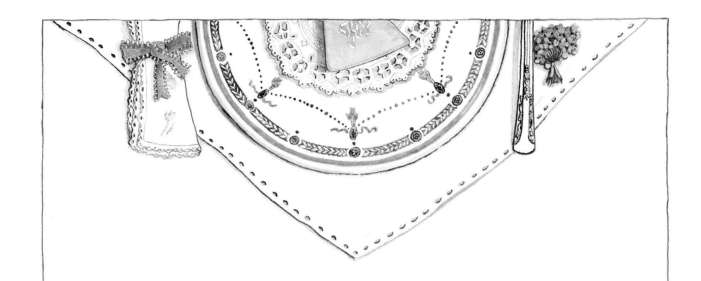

Orange Icing

zest of 1 orange   1½ c. powdered sugar
juice of 1 orange   1 tsp. white rum
          coconut for garnish (opt.)
          Lightly grate rind of orange & bring it & the juice
to a boil. Strain the juice & pour as much hot juice
over sugar as needed to make right consistency for
spreading. Stir in rum. ♥

To Assemble

          Put the chilled filling between layers. Frost with
orange icing, allowing some to dribble over edges.
Sprinkle on coconut if you like. The cake looks
beautiful served on plates lined with lace doilies. ♥

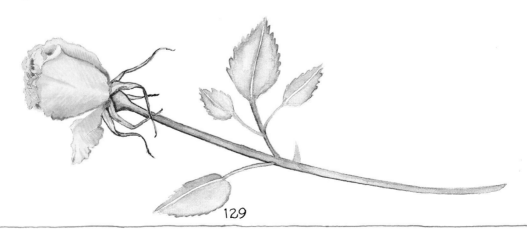

CHOCOLATE CAKE

350° Serves Eight

If you like a rich, dense, fudge-like cake with a texture almost like creamy peanut butter, this is the recipe for you ♥. Notice that it calls for no flour. ♥

16 oz. semi-sweet chocolate
1 c. unsalted butter
9 eggs, separated

1 c. sugar
unsweetened cocoa or
flour, for dusting

Preheat oven to 350°. Butter a 9" springform pan; line the bottom with buttered wax paper; dust pan with cocoa or flour. Slowly melt chocolate & butter together in a heavy saucepan over low heat; cool. Meanwhile separate eggs into two large bowls. Beat the yolks for about a minute; slowly add sugar & continue beating till thick & lemon-colored. Beat egg whites until they just begin to peak. Add cooled chocolate mixture to egg yolks & blend thoroughly. Pour the chocolate & yolk mixture into egg whites & fold gently until completely blended. Remove ⅓ of the batter to refrigerator & cover. Pour rest of batter into prepared pan & bake 40-45 minutes. Cool ½ hour before turning out onto serving plate. Frost with remaining batter. Garnishes include whipped cream, sliced almonds, sifted powdered sugar; all are optional. ♥ For Valentine's Day: cut out another round of wax paper & draw hearts on it; cut them out. Lay the paper on cake & sift powdered sugar over the top. Remove paper carefully. ♥

FUDGE

This recipe always comes out perfectly & without the use of a candy thermometer. Give it to someone special on Valentine's Day ~ it's a must at Christmastime ♥.

1 lg. can condensed milk
4 c. sugar
16 oz. semi~sweet chocolate bits

½ lb. sweet butter
chopped nuts of choice (opt)

Put the milk & sugar in a heavy pan. Bring to a boil. Start timing when boiling starts ~ cook 8½ minutes, stirring constantly. Put the chocolate bits & butter in a large bowl & pour the sugar mixture over. Mix with electric mixer, blending well. Stir in chopped nuts & spread in buttered pan to a depth of 1 inch. Partially chill & cut in squares with a hot knife. Refrigerate. ♥

"I wasn't kissing her, I was whispering in her mouth."
♥ Chico Marx

ALMOND BRITTLE

This makes a perfect candy for gift giving—especially good for mailing. But it comes with a warning: make it, get it packed, & get it OUT of the house. Sometimes I let it sit out cooling too long & somehow it's GONE before I get it sent. (DON'T LOOK AT ME ☺) ♥

You will need a candy thermometer for this.
2 c. sugar
1 lb. unsalted (sweet) butter
¼ c. water
10 oz. sliced almonds
8 oz. unsweetened chocolate

Combine sugar, butter, & water in large heavy pot. Stirring constantly, bring to a boil over moderately high heat. Occasionally dip a pastry brush in cold water & wash down sugar from sides of pan. Boil rapidly, stirring, till temperature reaches 295°. Remove from heat. Quickly stir in almonds & spread thinly on 2 cookie sheets. Melt the chocolate over very low heat. When candy is just slightly warm, almost cool, brush with melted chocolate. When chocolate has hardened, break into pieces & store in an airtight container. ♥

"Never eat more than you can lift."
Miss Piggy

INDIAN PUDDING

300° Serves Eight

An old New England favorite, this pudding is best served warm with a big scoop of vanilla ice cream. It's a comforting wintertime dessert. ♥

5½ c. whole milk	1 tsp. ginger
2/3 c. cornmeal	1 tsp. cinnamon
4 Tbsp. butter	½ tsp. salt
½ c. maple syrup	1 c. raisins
¼ c. molasses	vanilla ice cream

Preheat oven to 300°. Butter a small casserole ~ mine is 6½" × 10½". Over med. heat, in a large saucepan, heat the milk but don't boil it. Slowly whisk in cornmeal & continue to stir until mixture begins to thicken ~ 10 min. or so. Add remaining ingredients & keep stirring till heated through. Pour into casserole & bake 3 hours till sides are brown & sticky-looking. (The pudding hardens a bit as it cools.) Serve warm with vanilla ice cream. ♥

"No Spring, nor Summer Beauty
   hath such grace,
As I have seen in one Autumnall face."
   ♥ John Donne

BOURBON BALLS

Makes about 60

A delicious holiday candy. ♥

1 box powdered sugar, plus ⅓ c.	4 oz. unsweetened chocolate
1 stick butter, softened	1 oz. paraffin wax, grated
⅓ c. bourbon	1 box toothpicks

Sift 1 box powdered sugar over butter & cream together thoroughly. Stir in bourbon & put into freezer 5 min. Sift the ⅓ c. powdered sugar onto plate. Roll sugar mixture into 1" balls, then in powdered sugar. Place them onto cookie sheet & into freezer for 15 min. Stick a toothpick into each ball. Melt chocolate & paraffin together. Working quickly, dip each ball in chocolate; place on wax paper on cookie sheet. Remove picks. Reheat chocolate, then dribble a bit more on each candy to cover toothpick hole. Put them back in freezer 5 more min. Store in covered container in refrigerator. ♥

"Lost, yesterday, somewhere between sunrise and sunset, two golden hours, each set with sixty diamond minutes. No reward is offered, for they are gone forever."
♥ Horace Mann

OLD-FASHIONED APPLE PIE

450° Serves Eight

This is the kind of country pie they used to make in the "good old days"—with a tall top crust filled with juicy apples.

14 green apples, peeled, cored & sliced   1/4 tsp. salt
1 c. brown sugar   3½ Tbsp. cornstarch
1 tsp. cinnamon   1 Tbsp. lemon juice
½ tsp. nutmeg   2 Tbsp. butter

Combine all ingredients except butter. Pour into pie shell, piling high in the middle. Dot with butter. Cover with top crust. Cut out vents in top center. Bake on cookie sheet 10 min. at 450°, reduce heat to 350° & bake 40~50 min. longer till apples are tender & crust is brown. ♥

Pie Crust

4 c. unbleached flour.   2 c. Crisco shortening
2 tsp. salt   ice water to form ball

♥ Chill all ingredients—1 hr.

Put the flour & salt in a bowl & cut in Crisco with pastry cutter to the size of small peas. Slowly add ice water, stirring with fork till dough comfortably holds together in a ball. Flour a board & rolling pin. You'll need a bottom crust 1/8" thick & about 10" in diameter & a top crust of at least 16" in diameter. Divide dough accordingly & roll out bottom crust; put into 8" pie dish. Fill with apples; lay over top crust, fold & crimp edges. See above to finish. ♥

WITCHES' BREW
Makes 12 cups

This is a holiday brew made by GOOD witches ♥. It's really very elegant & is perfect for Halloween, Thanksgiving & Christmas parties. ♥

1 dozen eggs, separated
2/3 c. milk
1 c. sugar
pinch of salt
1¼ c. whipping cream, whipped

1 46 oz. can apricot nectar
1¼ c. brandy
⅓ c. Triple Sec
nutmeg

In the top part of double boiler, beat egg yolks well. Add the milk, ¾ c. sugar, & salt; cook over simmering water 20 min., stirring occasionally. Cool. Beat the egg whites till frothy, add ¼ c. sugar & continue beating till stiff. Whip the cream & pour into whites; pour cooled custard over all & gently fold till blended. Gently stir in nectar, brandy, & Triple Sec. Cover & refrigerate overnight. When ready to serve, beat it with a whisk, then pour into a punch bowl. Sprinkle with nutmeg & serve. Note: I have a Man-in-the-Moon mold 🌙 I use to make one big ice cube to put in at Halloween, & a star-shaped one for Christmas. It's not necessary, but it helps if the room is warm. ♥

"Nothing can be truer than
fairy wisdom. It is as true
as sunbeams." ♥ Douglas Jerrold

136

(Baked Alaska, or)
SNOWBALL IN HELL
450° Serves Six

Individual mountains of meringue covering ice cream & cake, quickly browned & served in a puddle of hot chocolate sauce. Easy! Perfect for Christmas Eve dinner. ♥

Meringue:
  4 egg whites
  6 Tbsp. powdered sugar
  pinch of salt
  1 tsp. vanilla

6 1" slices angel food
  cake
6 big scoops vanilla
  ice cream
Chocolate Sauce

First make the chocolate sauce. Preheat oven to 450°. Beat egg whites till stiff (not dry). Gradually beat in sugar, then add salt & vanilla. Put parchment paper on rimless cookie sheet. Lay out six slices cake about 3" x 3" each. Working quickly, place a big scoop of ice cream on each slice; spread meringue to cover ice cream & cake, making it look like a mountain 🏔. Bake 3~4 min. till browned. Slide off onto dishes & surround with a puddle of Chocolate Sauce. Serve. ♥

Chocolate Sauce

1½ Tbsp. butter
2 oz. unsweetened chocolate
⅓ c. boiling water

¾ c. sugar
3 Tbsp. corn syrup
1 Tbsp. rum

Melt butter & chocolate in heavy saucepan. Stir in boiling water, then sugar & syrup. Stirring, bring to boil. Boil softly 8~9 min. without stirring. Remove from heat; cool 15 min. Stir in rum. ♥

Orange Ice

Serves Four

Delicious and refreshing on its own, but for gorgeous color & more sophistication try it with Raspberry Sauce (p.139). ♥

3 c. fresh orange juice
½ c. sugar
½ c. lemon juice
grated rind of 2 oranges

Bring orange juice to boil. Stir in sugar till dissolved. Cool. Add lemon juice & rind. Freeze in hand-cranked or electric ice cream maker. You can also freeze it in a metal bowl, stir-ring every so often. Ices are best when served slightly mushy — not frozen stiff. ♥

Tip: The wonderful Donvier ice cream maker makes ice cream & ices in minutes with no electricity & no fuss. Get one. ♥

RASPBERRY SAUCE

Makes 1 cup

Spoon some of this beautiful red sauce onto a plate & set a scoop of Orange Ice (p.138) on top. Or try it with a slice of Chocolate Cake (p.130). Also good with ice cream and/or waffles. ♥

2 c. fresh (or frozen) raspberries
2 Tbsp. currant jelly
1–2 Tbsp. sugar
1 tsp. cornstarch

Crush the raspberries & force through sieve to remove seeds. Put the raspberry juice, along with the jelly, into a small saucepan & bring to a boil. Add sugar to taste; simmer 2 min. Mix the cornstarch with 1 Tbsp. cold water till smooth; slowly whisk mixture into sauce. Cook, stirring, 5–7 min. till thickened. Chill. ♥

CHOCOLATE MOUSSE

Serves Eight

I have a chocoholic girlfriend out in California who makes all other chocolate lovers pale by comparison. So I knew exactly who to go to when I wanted the most exquisite Chocolate Mousse possible. Very rich & chocolaty but uses no egg yolks as most recipes do. (Diana probably thinks it's diet food ♥.)

8-oz. semisweet chocolate   2-3 Tbsp. lukewarm water
¼ c. dark rum   2 egg whites
½ c. sugar   2 c. heavy cream

Melt chocolate in top of double boiler. Meanwhile cook rum & sugar over very low heat till sugar melts (do not let it brown). Add sugar syrup to chocolate (they should be about the same temp.). Beat in 2 Tbsp. lukewarm water; set aside. Beat egg whites till stiff; whip cream & fold together. Beat chocolate again — if it has thickened, add 1 more Tbsp. water. Fold chocolate into cream & spoon into individual serving dishes or wine glasses. Chill.

SWEET POTATO PIE

475° Serves Eight

This pie has a crunchy pecan topping & a smooth, spicy middle — good hot or cold; try it for Thanksgiving.

1 9 in. homemade pie shell	3 beaten eggs
1/2 c. chopped pecans	1 tsp. vanilla
2 c. cooked sweet potatoes	1/3 c. sugar
6 Tbsp. softened butter	1 tsp. cinnamon
1/4 c. heavy cream	1/2 tsp. nutmeg

Preheat oven to 475°. Make your favorite pie shell — prick all over with fork & spread pecans in bottom. Bake 5 min. Cool. Lower heat to 300°. Mash together potatoes & butter till smooth. Add all other ingredients & blend well. Pour into pie shell. Make the

Topping

3 Tbsp. melted butter	1/2 c. brown sugar
2/3 c. pecans, finely chopped	1/3 c. flour

Combine all ingredients till crumbly. Sprinkle over top of pie. Put the pie on a cookie sheet & bake at 300° for 25~30 min. till golden brown. Delicious with whipped cream or ice cream.

Tea

I am a tea drinker — I drink it every morning with honey & milk. I learned to drink it that way from my best friend Janet, & her English mom, Maisie. ♥

The first time I had a "real" English tea was in a beautiful old hotel in London. I walked in to the large room with its high ceilings & ornate moldings, massive windows (the rain was coming down hard), a fire in the huge fireplace & yellow roses everywhere. There was a grand piano & wonderful music & silver trays of delicate sandwiches, scones & biscuits, tiny cream puffs, cakes, & Napoleons. And pots of steaming hot tea. I was quite impressed! (wow)

But when it's tea time at home I usually don't make too much of a fuss — I feel like it's more a time for very close friends & family, kind of casual. My friends know to just drop in when they can. We usually have a plain cake or some nut bread & butter & I do serve the tea in the good China cups — even when I'm alone; I try to pay attention to the moment. I find myself more inclined in the winter afternoons, when it gets dark so early & there's a fire burning.

And once a winter I have my girlfriends over for a morning tea. First we trek out to the woods for a walk — then we settle in for Potato Heaven (p. 68), sausages cooked in maple syrup, and my grandma's Nut Bread (p.149). I encourage everyone to wear their most comfortable clothes & bring their slippers — so it's very cozy & not fussy at all. In front of the fire we drink tea & talk. ♥

Tea time is usually at 4 p.m. — it's a little interlude in the day & a quiet tradition. Recipes? Turn the page...

"The height of luxury was reached in the
winter afternoons . . . lying in a tin bath
in front of a coal fire, drinking tea,
and eating well-buttered crumpets. . . ."
♥ J. C. Masterman

ELAINE'S FAMOUS SUGAR COOKIES

325° Makes 7 dozen

A wonderful tea cookie — you can color the sugar for Christmas cookies. ♥ From my dear friend, Elaine Sullivan. ♥

1 c. butter, softened
1 c. powdered sugar
1 c. granulated sugar
2 eggs
1 c. salad oil
2 tsp. vanilla

1 tsp. grated lemon peel
4¼ c. flour
1 tsp. baking soda
1 tsp. cream of tartar
1 tsp. salt
plain or colored sugar

Cream butter & sugars; beat in eggs one at a time until light & fluffy. Beat in oil, vanilla & lemon peel. Combine dry ingredients & gradually add to sugar mixture, beating till well blended. Wrap in wax paper; chill several hours.

Preheat oven to 325°. Grease 2 cookie sheets. Divide dough into thirds (keep ⅓ out, refrigerate the rest till needed). Form heaping tsp. of dough into ball. Place on cookie sheet. Flatten to 2" diameter with bottom of glass dipped in sugar. Sprinkle with plain or colored sugar & bake 8~10 min. till lightly browned. Let stand on cookie sheet 2~3 min. before removing. ♥

"Every man's life is a fairy tale
written by God's fingers."
♥ Hans Christian Andersen

POPPY SEED CAKE

350°

This is sort of a plain cake, which, I think, is the charm of it. ♥

½ c. poppy seed
1 c. milk
1½ c. sugar
½ c. butter, softened
pinch of salt

1 tsp. vanilla
2 c. flour
2 tsp. baking powder
4 egg whites
powdered sugar

Soak poppy seed in milk for 1 hour. Preheat oven to 350°. Cream sugar & butter thoroughly. Add poppy seed with milk, salt, & vanilla. Stir in flour & baking powder. Beat egg whites stiffly & fold in. Pour into well-greased tube pan & bake 1 hour. Cool, turn out & sift over a little powdered sugar. ♥

"Optimism: A cheerful frame of mind
that enables a tea kettle to sing though
in hot water up to its nose."
                              Anonymous

Apple Muffins

400° Makes 12

The first big snowstorm hit this morning — it's clean & white outside. Writing about apple muffins helps to warm me, but I'd rather be eating them .

2 c. unbleached flour
3/4 tsp. salt
4 tsp. baking powder
1/4 c. sugar
1 tsp. cinnamon
4 Tbsp. butter

1 c. peeled apple, chopped
1/2 c. walnuts, chopped
3/4 c. milk
2 eggs
cinnamon & 2 Tbsp. sugar
12 apple rings, cored (use small apples)

Preheat oven to 400°. Mix together first 5 ingredients. Cut in butter with pastry blender. Add finely chopped apple & walnuts. Add milk to beaten eggs; stir into dry ingredients, just to moisten. Fill buttered muffin tins. Place an apple ring (unpeeled) on the top of each muffin & sprinkle tops with cinnamon mixed with 2 Tbsp. sugar to taste. Bake 20 min. Serve.

"To Debbie Pookie Poople Pigs from Petey Popsy Pooples — I love you — be mine."
 Valentine's message from the
<u>London Times</u>, 1982

MAPLE PECAN SCONES

400° Makes 10

Heart-shaped, they look wonderful for tea, for breakfast, or even with soup. Serve with marmalade, butter & jam. ♥

2 c. flour
1 Tbsp. baking powder
¼ tsp. soda
¼ tsp. salt
4 Tbsp. cold sweet butter

½ c. ground pecans
⅓ c. cream
¼ c. maple syrup
1 whole egg
1 egg yolk

Preheat oven to 400°. Stir dry ingredients together with a fork. Chop the butter into bits & cut it into dry ingredients till it resembles coarse meal. Stir in pecans. Combine cream, maple syrup & egg. Stir into dry ingredients, just enough to hold together in a ball. Turn onto floured board; knead 30 seconds. Pat dough to ½" thick. Cut with floured 3" heart-shaped cutter. Mix the egg yolk with 1 Tbsp. water & brush tops of scones. Bake 1" apart on buttered cookie sheet for 15 min. till golden brown. Serve. ♥

TEA CAKES & HONEY BUTTER

350° Makes 16

Old-fashioned, hot little cakes — make them for someone you love.

1 c. hot milk
½ c. butter
1 tsp. salt
½ c. sugar
1 pkg. dry yeast
¼ c. warm water

3 eggs
3½ c. flour
⅓ c. sugar
1½ tsp. cinnamon
butter, softened
honey

Preheat oven to 350°. In a lg. bowl, pour hot milk over butter, salt, & sugar. Cool to lukewarm. Dissolve yeast in warm water; allow to stand 5 min. Add the yeast & eggs to milk mixture, beating well. Gradually add flour & beat till smooth. Cover with cloth, let rise in warm place 1 hour. Fill buttered muffin tins ½ full. Combine sugar & cinnamon; sprinkle 1 tsp. over each muffin. Bake 20-25 min. Cream softened butter with honey to taste & serve with the warm cakes.

"The little old kitchen had quieted down from the bustle and confusion of mid-day; and now, with its afternoon manners on, presented a holiday aspect, that as the principal room in the brown house, it was eminently proper it should have."

Margaret Sidney

NUT BREAD

325° Makes 1 loaf

Such an easy bread! No kneading or waiting—also, no fat! Makes a beautiful loaf of bread, nice with tea, & a sweet homey Christmas present. It comes with love from my Grandma, Florence "Spitfire" Orr Smith.

2 c. flour	⅓ c. sugar
2 tsp. baking powder	1 egg, beaten
½ tsp. salt	1 c. milk

½ c. walnuts, chopped

Preheat oven to 325°. Mix dry ingredients together with a fork. Beat the egg, mix it with milk & pour into dry ingredients. Mix well; stir in nuts. Pour into buttered bread pan; bake 35 min. till toothpick comes out dry. Serve with softened butter. ♥

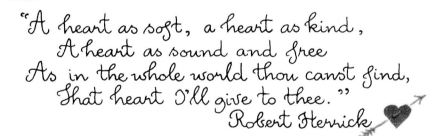

"A heart as soft, a heart as kind,
   A heart as sound and free
As in the whole world thou canst find,
   That heart I'll give to thee."
                    Robert Herrick

SANDWICHES

Use only the freshest of ingredients, the optimum in color, texture & flavor. For tea, crustless heart shapes, rounds & fingers look nice — you can arrange them on a paper doily if you like. If you are expecting weekend guests, a large platter of different sandwiches ready & waiting in the fridge comes in real handy. We never go to the beach without our cucumber sandwiches for sustenance. ♥

CUCUMBER : Cut rounds from good white bread, spread with mayonnaise, add thin slices peeled cucumber, salt & pepper. Spread sandwich edge with the thinnest coat of mayonnaise & roll edge in minced parsley. Chill. ♥

TOMATO: On fresh pumpernickel rounds, spread mayonnaise, add thin slices cherry tomato, salt & pepper, then fresh basil leaves. Chill. ♥

AVOCADO: Toast one side crustless wheat bread — spread mayonnaise on untoasted side, add avocado, pepper & salt, then sprouts. Cut into squares. Serve P.D.Q. ♥

NASTURTIUM: Spread white bread heart shapes with cream cheese, add fresh nasturtiums. ♥

RADISH: Slice French bread baguette, spread with sweet butter, add thick slices radish, pepper & serve open-faced. ♥

SANDWICHES

NOTE: For a baby shower, your bakery will add food coloring to bread, making it pink or blue. ♥ Looks terrible ♡, tastes just fine & certainly is festive. For Christmas buffet, do red & green.

CHICKEN: Finely chop cooked chicken, celery, walnuts. Mix with mayonnaise, add a bit of curry to taste. Spread on good white bread cut into finger shapes. Chill. ♥

CHEESE: Sharp cheddar on white bread with mustard & sliced sweet pickles. ♥

PEANUT BUTTER & JELLY: I like "extra crunchy" & lots of jelly. These should be heart-shaped & on white bread. ♥

HAPPY BIRTHDAY!

As the oldest of 8 children I have memories of many wonderful birthday parties. I think my mom must be the all-time expert on how to make a birthday special but then she made every day special for us ♥. On rainy days she'd let us turn the entire house into an underground maze of a tent ~ with the use of blankets, clothespins & various pieces of furniture we would have a castle. The only room that was off-limits was the kitchen, where on cold mornings she would close all the doors, turn on the oven to heat the room & fill the basinet with warm water in which she'd bathe "our" baby. It was cozy-warm & my little brother or sister was always fat & pink & slippery. I loved to help ~ my mom & I played "dolls" together with real babies ♥.

For birthday parties she would make wonderful creative cakes ~ sometimes we'd find dimes inside but my favorite was the "Circus Cake." It had candy canes stuck in the top holding up a pointed construction paper "roof" and animal crackers pressed into the pink frosting all around the sides. The whole thing was sprinkled with colored candies & we thought our mom was a genius. ♥

Here are some other birthday suggestions:

Sparklers make the cake look wonderful for your adult friends ~ no candles for unpleasant reminders! Don't forget to turn off the lights & sing LOUD.

Tuck something special ~ even just a little note ~ into lunch box, briefcase, pockets or purse. ♥

DAD Birthday banners are fun ~ put them up along the travel route of the honored one. Say things like "Smile, Janet! It's your Birthday!!" ♥

Try a "Backwards Party." Everyone wears his clothes backwards; the invitation must be read by holding it up to a mirror, and the meal should start with dessert. ♥

Balloons, banners, hats, noisemakers, special invitations, placecards, crepe paper twists, nutcups & confetti bring birthday smiles to children of all ages. ♥

Have a "treasure hunt" for your children. Hide peanuts all over the yard ~ give each child a bag with his name on it ~ give them about 10 minutes from the GO! Have a prize for whoever finds the most nuts. ♥

Every child should go home with a "prize." Have a grab bag with small wrapped toys, one for the boys & one for the girls. Everyone should have a balloon, too. ♥

Don't forget to take lots of pictures. ♥

When you're out & about & you see some-thing special that doesn't cost an arm & a leg ~ BUY it. You'll always have a stock of presents for emergencies ♥.

EPILOGUE

'Been writing & cooking a year now or more,
  and now that I'm finished, I'm ready to soar.
But lo & behold, ten pounds have appeared;
  my tummy looks fat & my rear end looks weird!
I'm planning a visit to old friends out west;
  wishing & hoping that I'll look my best.
So it's sit-ups & leg-lifts from now on for me
  and one thing I promise, I will guarantee
That the next book I write, the next book you see
  will be veggies & health food & mostly fat free! ❤

FRIENDS

"To get the full value
of a Joy
You must have Somebody
to divide it with."
Mark Twain ♥

Special thanks to the "Somebodies" who stood by me with encouragement, diversion, and love. To Valerie Reese, who cooked up a storm while I painted, & made sure it all came out all right with the use of measuring cups & spoons! ♥ To Randi Russell & her new baby, Raleigh, for the experiences we share. ♥ And, most of all, to Joe Hall, my handsome "6'2" Leo who can cook" for believing me when I promised that after this, I'll make dinner. ♥

And it wouldn't be right if I forgot to mention Man Cat, Girl Cat, & Wm. T. Aristocat (Bill) for their contributions: walking across my pages with kitty feet was only one of the ideas they had to "help". ♥

155

INDEX

" Out of the strain of the Doing,
Into the race of the Done. "
♥ Julia Woodruff